بسم الله الرحمن الرحيم

O Mankind: Worship your Lord, Who created you and all those before you, so that you might be God-fearing (la'allakum tattaqūn).

(al-Baqarah 2: 21)

Mankind

A Pocketful of Gems from the Qu'ran

Compiled by

Umm Fahtima Zahra

O Mankind: A Pocketful of Gems from the Qur'an

First published in England by
Kube Publishing Ltd
Markfield Conference Centre,
Ratby Lane, Markfield,
Leicestershire, LE67 9SY,
United Kingdom
Tel: +44 (0) 1530 249230
Email: info@ kubepublishing.com
Website: www.kubepublishing.com

CIP data for this book is available from the British Library.

ISBN: 978-0-86037-813-6 Paperback
ISBN: 978-0-86037-888-4 ebook

Cover Design and typesetting by: Afreen Fazil (Jaryah Studios)

Printed by: IMAK, Turkey

For my beloved parents, loving husband and my most precious gems.

May Allah ﷻ grant you an eternal and magnificent abode in the Hereafter, together in the Gardens of al-Firdaws, āmīn.

O Allah! Send blessings and peace upon Muhammad ﷺ and the family of Muhammad ﷺ. Āmīn.

And when My servants ask you of Me, truly I am near; I answer the prayer of the supplicant when he calls on Me. So let them truly answer Me, and believe in Me, that they may be rightly guided.

(*al-Baqarah*, 2: 186)

Contents

Introduction 1

Glorifying Allah ﷻ 5

Praising Allah ﷻ 23

Invocations of Peace and Blessings on the Prophet ﷺ 29

The Precious Gems 35

The Tenets of Faith 36

Seeking Protection from The Shayatin (Devils) 42

Seeking Protection from Black Magic, Witchcraft & the Evil Eye 43

Du'*ā* for the Acceptance of One's Worship ('Ibadah) 45

Du'ā for Guidance and Assistance 45

Seeking Refuge from Ignorance and Wrongdoing 48

Du'ā for a Distinguished Reward 49

Du'ā for Rizq (Sustenance) 49

Seeking Goodness in this World and the Hereafter and Protection from the Fire 50

Du'ā to Inherit Paradise 52

Seeking Protection from The Fire 53

Du'ā for Light and Safety on the Day of Judgement and on the Bridge-over-Hell (al-Sirat) 54

Du'ā for Wisdom and Piety 55

Du'ā When Reaching the Age of Forty 56
Du'ā to Increase in Knowledge 57
Du'ā for Confidence and Contentment 57
Du'ā for Ease 58
Du'ā for Clarity of Speech 58
Supplicating to Allah ﷻ to Reveal the Truth 59
Seeking a Sign From Allah ﷻ 60
Du'ā For Righteous Children 60
Du'ā for Righteous Spouses and Offspring 62
Du'ā After Giving Birth 63
Du'ā for Guidance and Righteousness 63
Du'ā For Parents 66
Du'ā in Times of Trial 67
Du'ā When Afflicted with a Calamity 68
Du'ā when in Distress and Pain 69
Seeking Help when Overburdened 70
Seeking Protection from Oppressors 72
To Avoid Confrontation for the Sake of Allah ﷻ 74
Special Protection (being veiled by Allah ﷻ) 74
To Overcome an Oppressor; Oppressive Ruler & Seeking Patience 75
Du'ā for Justice 76

Du'ā: Allah ﷻ Never Breaks His Promise.....77

Trust in and Reliance on Allah ﷻ 78

Du'ā when on a Journey.....83

Asking for Security for One's Land & Guidance for One's Children.....85

Asking for Security for One's Land and for Sustenance.....85

Du'ā for Constant Glorification, Gratitude & Remembrance of Allah ﷻ.....86

Du'ā when Thanking Allah ﷻ.....88

Invocations for Forgiveness.....91

Seeking Allah's Forgiveness.....92

Repentance of the Prophets ﷺ.....95

A Concluding Prayer.....101

Transliteration

Arabic Alphabet and their English Equivalents

J	ج	Th	ث	T	ت	b	ب	a	ا
R	ر	Dh	ذ	D	د	kh	خ	ḥ	ح
ḍ	ض	ṣ	ص	Sh	ش	s	س	Z/z	ز
F	ف	Gh	غ	‘/’a	ع	ẓ	ظ	ṭ	ط
N	ن	M	م	L	ل	k	ك	q	ق
‘	ء	T	ة	I	ى	w	و	h	ه

ﷻ Used following the mention of Allah translated as “Glory be to Allah.”

ﷺ Used following the mention of the Messenger of Allah, Muhammad, translated as “May Allah bless him and grant him peace.”

عليه السلام/عليها السلام/عليهم السلام Used following the mention of the honourable Prophets, Messengers and other noble and holy figures etc, translated as “May the peace of Allah be upon him/her/them.”

رضي الله عنه/رضي الله عنها/رضي الله عنهم Used following the mention of a Companion or Companions of the Prophet, a disciple or disciples of Isa, and other pious personalities, translated as “May Allah be pleased with him”, “May Allah be pleased with her” and “May Allah be pleased with them”.

Foreword

Bismi Allāhi al-Raḥmāni al-Raḥīm. In the name of Allah, the Most Merciful the Compassionate.

By Allah's great favour, I was given the opportunity to complete this project, *alḥamdullilāh*, after looking in numerous bookshops around the world and also online and not finding a comprehensive compilation of Du'ā's taken from the Qur'an.

Before I embarked on compiling these supplications, whenever I read the *musḥaf*, beautiful gems glistened and sparkled as I turned page after page of the Qur'an, which I used to scribble down quickly on a piece of paper. This happened at a difficult period when I was going through testing times and hardship, and asking Allah ﷻ for ease and relief. Later on, I decided to compile these gems of incredible wisdom in a pocketbook.

After all, the Prophets, Messengers (peace be upon them all), and other Noble women whom Allah ﷻ speaks about in the Qur'an also suffered hardships, more intense than any hardship that any one of us may ever suffer.

I hope that this compilation helps the readers in everyday life and that the most perfect words of Allah ﷻ grant them tranquility of heart and guide them to every success in this world and the next.

Peace and blessings be upon our Prophet Muhammad ﷺ, his family, Companions and all of you.

To Allah we belong and to Him is our return. May Allah ﷻ forgive us all. *Āmīn*.

Umm Fahtima Zahra

Ramadan 1443 AH

بِسۡمِ ٱللَّهِ ٱلرَّحۡمَٰنِ ٱلرَّحِيمِ

Bismi Allāhi al-Raḥmāni al-Raḥīm

In the name of Allah Most Gracious Merciful and Compassionate

Introduction

Allah ﷻ has sent us a glorious book that illustrates, among many other things, the ways to make *du'ā* to Him, may He be exalted and praised.

This handbook provides a pocketful of glistening gems from the Qur'an that one can use in one's daily life.

It highlights how to beseech and glorify Allah ﷻ in the most perfect manner; with a variety of powerful hadiths regarding sending peace and blessings upon the Messenger of Allah ﷺ, and additional prayers specifically taught by Allah, the Most Wise.

Allah ﷻ and His Messenger Muhammad ﷺ have instructed the believers on the best manner to ask of Him.

Fudalah ibn 'Ubayd ﷺ reported that the Messenger of Allah ﷺ said: "When anyone of you makes du'ā, let him start by glorifying his Lord and praising Him, then let him send blessings upon the Prophet ﷺ, then let him pray for whatever he wants." (Abū Dāwūd, #1481, al-Tirmidhī, #3477)

If one takes this hadith and break it into different components, one can perfect the way one makes *du'ā* as taught by the Messenger of Allah ﷺ.

The different components of this hadith are as follows:

1. "Start by glorifying his Lord" – and Part One of this pocketbook will provide a variety of ways to sanctify our Lord with words taken from the Qur'an.

2. "And praising Him" - Part Two presents a selection of illustrative prayers that different Prophets of Allah used to praise Allah ﷻ as related in the Qur'an.

3. "Then let him send blessings upon the Prophet ﷺ" - Part Three provides a series of salutations upon the Prophet ﷺ from Hadith. Sending salutations upon the Prophet ﷺ before any prayer is like wrapping one's *du'ā* in perfect gold and presenting it to one's Sublime and Most Generous Lord, Allah.

   Allah ﷻ says in the Qur'an:

   Allah and His angels bless the Prophet. O You who believe, invoke blessing and peace upon him, (al-Aḥzāb, 33:56)

4. "Then let him pray for whatever he wants" - Part Four introduces a series of du'as from the Qur'an for different occasions. These supplications were made by Noble Prophets, their wives, Messengers, the people of Paradise and some Noble Women of Islam.

5. Muslims are also advised to seek forgiveness from their Lord.

   'And ask forgiveness of your Lord, and turn to Him in repentence. Verily my Lord is all-compassionate, ever tenderly loving-kind'. (Hūd, 11: 90)

These *Du'ā's* can be found in Part Five. By combining these five components, one can address Allah ﷻ with as near perfect supplications as possible. Allah ﷻ also teaches the believers and guides them on how to make their supplications accepted:

Their sides vacate their beds to supplicate to their Lord in fear and hope; and they spend out of what We have provided them. (al-Sajdah, 32: 16)

Call only on your Lord, with humility and in secret. Verily He loves not the transgressors. (al-A'rāf, 7: 55)

From this, one learns to make sincere supplications through being in a state of fear and hope, in secret, with humility and also to give charity to enhance one's *du'ā's* in the hope they will be accepted. The best guidance is the book of Allah, the Qur'an, and the best example is that of the Prophet Muhammad ﷺ.

Part One

Glorifying Allah ﷻ
A Collection of His Names and Attributes

قُلْ هُوَ ٱللَّهُ أَحَدٌ ١ ٱللَّهُ ٱلصَّمَدُ ٢ لَمْ يَلِدْ وَلَمْ يُولَدْ ٣
وَلَمْ يَكُن لَّهُۥ كُفُوًا أَحَدٌ ٤

Qul huwa 'llāhu aḥad Allāhuṣ-ṣamad Lam yalid wa-lam yūlad wa-lam yakun lahū kufuwan aḥad

Say, 'He is Allah, the One. Allah, Who is in need of none and of Whom all are in need. He neither begot any, nor was He begotten, and none is comparable to Him.'

(*Al-Ikhlas*, 112: 1-4)

هُوَ اللَّهُ الْخَالِقُ الْبَارِئُ الْمُصَوِّرُ لَهُ الْأَسْمَاءُ الْحُسْنَىٰ يُسَبِّحُ لَهُ مَا فِي السَّمَاوَاتِ وَالْأَرْضِ وَهُوَ الْعَزِيزُ الْحَكِيمُ

Huwa'llāhu al-khāliqu al-bāri'u al-muṣawwiru lahu'l-'asmā'u'l-ḥusnā yusabbiḥu lahu mā-fi'l-samāwāti wa'l-arḍi wa-huwa'l-'azīzu'l-ḥakīm

"He is Allah, the Creator, the Flawless Originator, the Bestower of Forms. His are the most beautiful names. Everything in the heavens and earth extol His incomparable glory, and He is the Invincible, the All-wise."

(*al-Ḥashr*, 59: 24)

هُوَ اللَّهُ الَّذِي لَا إِلَٰهَ إِلَّا هُوَ الْمَلِكُ الْقُدُّوسُ السَّلَامُ الْمُؤْمِنُ الْمُهَيْمِنُ الْعَزِيزُ الْجَبَّارُ الْمُتَكَبِّرُ سُبْحَانَ اللَّهِ عَمَّا يُشْرِكُونَ

Huwa'llāhu'l-ladhī lā ilāha illā huwa'l-maliku'l-quddūsu'l-salāmu'l-mu'minu'l-muhayminu'l-'azīzu'l-jabbāru'l-mutakabbiru subḥana'llāhi 'ammā yushrikūn

"He is Allah whom there is no god besides, the King, the Sacredly Pure, the the Source and Perfection of peace, the All-protecting, the One in charge of All, the Invincible, the Indomitable Conqueror, the Supreme on High: Glorious is Allah in perfection above all they join with Him in worship."

(*al-Ḥashr*, 59: 23)

هُوَ الْأَوَّلُ وَالْآخِرُ وَالظَّاهِرُ وَالْبَاطِنُ وَهُوَ بِكُلِّ شَيْءٍ عَلِيمٌ

Huwa'l-awwalu wa'l-ākhiru wa'l-ẓāhiru wa'l-bātinu
wa huwa bi-kulli shay'in 'alīm

"He is the First and the Last, and the Obvious and the Hidden, and He is the All-Knower of every single thing."

(*al-Ḥadīd*, 57: 3)

وَلَهُ الْكِبْرِيَاءُ فِي السَّمَاوَاتِ وَالْأَرْضِ وَهُوَ الْعَزِيزُ الْحَكِيمُ

Wa-lahu'l-kibriyā'u fi'l-samāwāti wa'l-arḍi
wa huwa'l-'azīzu'l-ḥakīm

"And His is the utter Supremacy in the heavens and earth; and He is the All-Mighty, the All-Wise."

(*al-Jāthiyah*, 45: 37)

لَهُ مَقَالِيدُ السَّمَاوَاتِ وَالْأَرْضِ يَبْسُطُ الرِّزْقَ لِمَن يَشَاءُ وَيَقْدِرُ
إِنَّهُ بِكُلِّ شَيْءٍ عَلِيمٌ

Lahu maqālīdu al-samāwāti wa'l-arḍi yabsuṭu al-rizqa li-man yashā'u wa yaqdiru innahu bi-kulli shay'in 'alīm

"To Him belong the keys of the heavens and earth; He outspreads provision to whomever He wills, and withholds in exact due measure; verily He is the All-Knower of every single thing."

(*al-Shūrā*, 42: 12)

وَمَا مِنْ إِلَٰهٍ إِلَّا اللَّهُ الْوَاحِدُ الْقَهَّارُ

Wa-mā min ilāhin illā'llāhu'l-wāḥidu'l-qahhār

"And no god is there but Allah, the One, the Indomitable Conqueror of All."

(*Ṣād*, 38: 65)

رَبُّ السَّمَاوَاتِ وَالْأَرْضِ وَمَا بَيْنَهُمَا الْعَزِيزُ الْغَفَّارُ

Rabbu'l-samāwāti wa'l-arḍi wa-mā baynahumā'l-'azīzu'l-ghaffār

"Lord of the heavens and the earth and all between them, the Invincible, the Oft-forgiving."

(*Ṣād*, 38: 66)

سُبْحَانَ اللَّهِ عَمَّا يَصِفُونَ

Subḥāna'llāhi 'ammā yaṣifūn

"Allah be high exalted above all they describe."

(*al-Ṣāffāt*, 37: 159)

الحَمدُ لِلَّهِ الَّذى لَهُ ما فِى السَّماواتِ وَما فِى الأَرضِ وَلَهُ الحَمدُ
فِى الآخِرَةِ وَهُوَ الحَكيمُ الخَبيرُ

Al-ḥamdu li-llāhi al-ladhī lahu mā-fī'l-samāwāti wa-mā fī'l-ardi wa-lahu al-ḥamdu fī'l-ākhirati wa-huwa al-ḥakīmu'l-khabīr

"All praise be to Allah who possesses all in the heavens and all on earth; and His alone is the praise on the next world; and He is the All-wise, the All-aware."

(*Saba'*, 34: 1)

يَعلَمُ ما يَلِجُ فِى الأَرضِ وَما يَخرُجُ مِنها وَما يَنزِلُ مِنَ السَّماءِ
وَما يَعرُجُ فيها وَهُوَ الرَّحيمُ الغَفورُ

Ya'lamu mā yaliju fī'l-arḍi wa-mā yakhruju minhā wa-mā yanzilu mina'l-samā'i wa-mā ya'ruju fīhā wa-huwa'l-raḥīmu'l-ghafūr

"He knows what disappears into the earth and what comes forth from it; and what descends from the sky and what rises up at a mighty incline into it; and He is the All-compassionate, the All-forgiving."

(*Saba'*, 34: 2)

إِنَّ ٱللَّهَ عِندَهُۥ عِلْمُ ٱلسَّاعَةِ وَيُنَزِّلُ ٱلْغَيْثَ وَيَعْلَمُ مَا فِى ٱلْأَرْحَامِ
وَمَا تَدْرِى نَفْسٌ مَّاذَا تَكْسِبُ غَدًا وَمَا تَدْرِى نَفْسٌۢ بِأَىِّ
أَرْضٍ تَمُوتُ إِنَّ ٱللَّهَ عَلِيمٌ خَبِيرٌ

Inna'llāha 'indahu 'ilmu'l-sā'ati wa-yunazzilu'l-ghaytha wa-ya'lamu mā-fī'l-arḥāmi wa-mā tadrī nafsun mādhā taksibu ghadan wa-mā tadrī nafsun bi-ayyi arḍin tamūtu inna'llāha 'alīmun khabīr

"Verily, Allah alone possesses knowledge of the Final Hour, and He alone sends down life-restoring rain; and He alone knows all yet hidden in wombs; and no soul can tell what it may earn tomorrow; and no soul can tell where on earth it will die: Verily Allah is all-knowing, all-aware."

(*Luqmān*, 31:34)

سُبْحَٰنَهُۥ وَتَعَٰلَىٰ عَمَّا يُشْرِكُونَ

Subḥānahu wa-ta'ālā 'ammā yushrikūn

"Glorious is He beyond compare and exalted above all they conjoin with Him in worship."

(*al-Rūm*, 30: 40)

ج لِلَّهِ الأَمرُ مِن قَبلُ وَمِن بَعدُ

Li'llāhi'l-amru min qablu wa-min ba'd

"Allah's is the decision, both ever before and forever after."

(*al-Rūm*, 30: 4)

الْحَمْدُ لِلَّهِ

Al-ḥamdu li'llāh

"All praise be to Allah!"

(*al-'Ankabūt*, 29: 63)

إِنَّكَ كُنتَ بِنَا بَصِيرا

Innaka kunta binā basīrā

"Verily You have always watched over us."

(*Ṭa-Ha*, 20: 35)

الْحَمْدُ لِلَّهِ الَّذِى لَمْ يَتَّخِذْ وَلَدًا وَلَم يَكُن لَّهُ شَرِيكٌ فِى الْمُلْكِ
وَلَمْ يَكُن لَّهُ وَلِىٌّ مِّنَ الذُّلِّ وَكَبِّرْهُ تَكْبِيرًا

Al-ḥamdu li'llāhi'l-ladhī lam yattakhidh waladan wa-lam yakun'lahu sharīkun fī'l-mulki wa-lam yakun lahu waliyyun mina'l-dhulli wa-kabbirhu takbīrā

"All praise is Allah's, who has never taken any offspring, nor had any partner in rule, nor out of abject helplessness needed any protector; and magnify Him with utter exaltation."

(*al-Isrā'*, 17: 111)

اللَّهُ خَالِقُ كُلِّ شَىْءٍ وَهُوَ الْوَاحِدُ الْقَهَّارُ

Allāhu khāliqu kulli shay'in wa-huwa'l-wāḥidu'l-qahhār

"Allah is the Creator of everything; and He is the One, the Indomitable Conqueror of All."

(*al-Ra'd*, 13: 16)

وَلِلّهِ غَيْبُ السَّمَاوَاتِ وَالأَرْضِ وَإِلَيْهِ يُرْجَعُ الأَمْرُ كُلُّهُ

Wa-li'llāhi ghaybu'l-samāwāti wa'l-arḍi wa-ilayhi yurja'u'l-amru kulluh

"And Allah alone possesses the unseen of the heavens and earth; and to Him the entire matter returns."

(*Hūd*, 11: 123)

وَإِن تَوَلَّوا فَاعلَموا أَنَّ اللَّهَ مَولاكُم ۚ نِعمَ المَولىٰ وَنِعمَ النَّصيرُ

Wa-in tawallaw fa-'lamū anna'llāha mawlākum ni'ma'l-mawlā wa-ni'ma'l-naṣīr

"And if they turn away, know that Allah is your Supreme Master; how splendid a master and splendid an ally!"

(*al-Anfāl*, 8: 40)

تَبَارَكَ اللّٰهُ رَبُّ الْعَالَمِينَ

Tabāraka'llāhu rabbu al-'ālamīn

"How gloriously exalted is Allah: Lord of all worlds of Beings!"

(*al-A'rāf*, 7: 54)

إِنَّ الْفَضْلَ بِيَدِ اللّٰهِ يُؤْتِيهِ مَن يَشَاء وَاللّٰهُ وَاسِعٌ عَلِيمٌ

Inna'l-faḍla bi-yadi'llāhi yu'tīhi man yashā'u wa'llāhu wāsi'un 'alīm

"Verily all favour is in the hand of Allah: He bestows it on whomever He wills, and Allah is vast of bounty, all-knowing."

(*Āl 'Imrān*, 3: 73)

تُولِجُ اللَّيْلَ فِي النَّهَارِ وَتُولِجُ النَّهَارَ فِي اللَّيْلِ وَتُخْرِجُ الْحَيَّ مِنَ الْمَيِّتِ وَتُخْرِجُ الْمَيِّتَ مِنَ الْحَيِّ وَتَرْزُقُ مَن تَشَاءُ بِغَيْرِ حِسَابٍ

Tūliju al-layla fī'l-nahāri wa-tūliju'l-nahāra fī'l-layli wa-tukhriju'l-ḥayya mina'l-mayyiti wa-tukhriju'l-mayyita mina'l-ḥayyi wa-tarzuqu man tashā'u bi-ghayri ḥisāb

"You enter the dark of night into where the very day was, and enter the dawning day into the departing night; and bring forth the living from the dead, and the dead from the living, and unfailingly provide for whom You will without reckoning."

(*Āl 'Imrān*, 3: 27)

اللَّهُ وَلِيُّ الَّذِينَ آمَنُواْ يُخْرِجُهُم مِّنَ الظُّلُمَاتِ إِلَى النُّوُرِ وَالَّذِينَ
كَفَرُواْ أَوْلِيَآؤُهُمُ الطَّاغُوتُ يُخْرِجُونَهُم مِّنَ النُّورِ إِلَى
الظُّلُمَاتِ أُوْلَـئِكَ أَصْحَابُ النَّارِ هُمْ فِيهَا خَالِدُونَ

Allāhu waliyyu'l-ladhīna āmanū yukhrijuhum mina'l-ẓulumāti ilā'l-nūri wa'l-ladhīna kafāru awliyā'uhumu'l-tāghūtu yukhrijūnahum mina'l-nūri ilā'l-ẓulumāti ūlā'ika aṣḥābu'l-nāri hum fīhā khālidūn.

"Allah Himself is the faithful protecting friend of all who shall believe, He brings them out of the deepest darkness into light, and those who disbelieve, their protectors are the abomination of idols: They take them out of the light into deepest darkness; those are the dwellers of the hellfire, in it shall they abide."

(*al-Baqarah*, 2: 257)

اللَّهُ لاَ إِلَـهَ إِلاَّ هُوَ الْحَيُّ الْقَيُّومُ لاَ تَأْخُذُهُ سِنَةٌ وَلاَ نَوْمٌ لَّهُ مَا فِي السَّمَاوَاتِ وَمَا فِي الأَرْضِ مَن ذَا الَّذِي يَشْفَعُ عِنْدَهُ إِلاَّ بِإِذْنِهِ يَعْلَمُ مَا بَيْنَ أَيْدِيهِمْ وَمَا خَلْفَهُمْ وَلاَ يُحِيطُونَ بِشَيْءٍ مِّنْ عِلْمِهِ إِلاَّ بِمَا شَاء وَسِعَ كُرْسِيُّهُ السَّمَاوَاتِ وَالأَرْضَ وَلاَ يَؤُودُهُ حِفْظُهُمَا وَهُوَ الْعَلِيُّ الْعَظِيمُ

Allāhu lā ilāha illā huwa'l-ḥayyu'l-qayyūmu lā ta'khūdhuhu sinatun wa-lā nawmun lahu mā-fī'l-samāwāti wa-mā fī'l-arḍi man dhā'l-ladhī yashfa'u 'indahu illā bi-idhnihi ya'lamu mā bayna aydīhim wa-mā khalfahum wa-lā yuḥīṭūna bi-shay'in min 'ilmihi illā bi-mā shā'a wasi'a kursiyyuhu'l-samāwāti wa-l-arda wa-lā ya'ūduhu ḥifẓuhumā wa-huwa'l-'aliyyu al-'aẓīm.

"Allah, no god is there but He, the Living, the Everlasting Source of All Being, slumber nor sleep overtake Him, His is all that is in the heavens and all on earth. Who should ever intercede with Him save by His leave? He knows all that takes place before their eyes and what lies yet unknown beyond them, and they encompass nothing of His knowledge, but what He wills, His Dominion compasses the heavens and earth, and preserving them burdens Him not, and He is the All-high, the Incomparably Supreme."

(*al-Baqarah*, 2: 255)

فَاعْلَمُوا أَنَّ اللَّهَ عَزِيزٌ حَكِيمٌ

Fa'lamū anna'llāha 'Azīzun Ḥakīm.

"Then know well that Allah is Invincible, Supreme in wisdom."

(*al-Baqarah*, 2: 209)

وَاللَّهُ رَؤُوفٌ بِالْعِبَادِ

Wa'llāhu Ra'ūfun bi'l-'ibād.

"And Allah is Gracious and tender towards servants."

(*al-Baqarah*, 2: 207)

إِنَّ اللَّهَ سَمِيعٌ عَلِيمٌ

Inna'llāha Samī'un 'Alīm.

"Verily Allah is All-Hearing, All-Knowing."

(*al-Baqarah*, 2: 181)

إِنَّ اللَّهَ غَفُورٌ رَّحِيمٌ

Inna'llāha Ghafūrun Raḥīm.

"Truly Allah is Oft-Forgiving, All-Compassionate."

(*al-Baqarah*, 2: 182)

وَإِلَـهُكُمْ إِلَهٌ وَاحِدٌ لاَّ إِلَهَ إِلاَّ هُوَ الرَّحْمَنُ الرَّحِيمُ

Wa-ilāhukum ilāhun wāḥidun lā ilāha illā huwa'l-Raḥmānu'l-Raḥīm.

"And your god is but One God, no god is there but He, the Most Merciful and Compassionate."

(*al-Baqarah*, 2: 163)

بَدِيعُ السَّمَاوَاتِ وَالأَرْضِ وَإِذَا قَضَى أَمْراً فَإِنَّمَا
يَقُولُ لَهُ كُن فَيَكُونُ

Badī'u'l-samāwāti wa'l-arḍi wa-idhā qada amran fa'innamā yaqūlu lahu kun fayakūn

"Originator of the heavens and earth: When He decrees a thing, He but tells it: 'Be!' and it is."

(*al-Baqarah*, 2: 117)

سُبْحَانَكَ لاَ عِلْمَ لَنَا إِلاَّ مَا عَلَّمْتَنَا إِنَّكَ أَنتَ الْعَلِيمُ الْحَكِيمُ

Subḥānaka lā 'ilma lanā illā mā 'allamtanā innaka anta al-'Alīmu al-ḥakīm.

"Glory be to you, we know naught but what You have taught us; verily You alone are the All-Knowing, the All-Wise."

(*al-Baqarah*, 2:32)

Part Two

Praising Allah ﷻ

قُلْ كُلٌّ مِنْ عِنْدِ اللّٰهِ

Qul Kullun min 'indi'llāh.

"Say: 'All things are from Allah."

(*al-Nisā'*, 4: 78)

الحَمدُ لِلَّهِ الَّذى هَدانا لِهٰذا وَما كُنّا لِنَهتَدِىَ لَولا أَن هَدانَا اللَّهُ ۖ لَقَد جاءَت رُسُلُ رَبِّنا بِالحَقِّ

Al-ḥamdu li-llāhi'l-ladhī hadānā li-hadhā wa-mā kunnā li-nahtadiya lawlā an hadānā'llāhu laqad jā'at rusulu rabbinā bi'l-ḥaqq.

"All praise be to Allah, who guided us for the sake of this; While never had we been guided, had Allah guided us not, verily the Messengers of our Lord brought the Truth."

(*al-A'rāf*, 7: 43)

وَلَم أَكُن بِدُعائِكَ رَبِّ شَقِيًّا

Wa-lam akun bi-Du'ā'ika rabbi shaqiyyā.

"Nor ever have I been in calling on You, my Lord, disappointed."

Prophet Zachariah ﷺ (*Maryam*, 19: 4)

الحَمدُ لِلَّهِ الَّذى نَجّانا مِنَ القَومِ الظّالِمينَ

Al-ḥamdu li'llāhi'l-ladhī najjāna mina'l-qawmi'l-ẓālimīn

"All praise is Allah's, who has truly delivered us from the wrongdoing lot."

Prophet Nuh ﷺ (*al-Mu'minūn*, 23: 28)

الْحَمْدُ لِلَّهِ الَّذِى فَضَّلَنَا عَلَى كَثِيرٍ مِّنْ عِبَادِهِ الْمُؤْمِنِينَ

*Al-ḥamdu li'llāhi'l-ladhī faḍalanā 'alā kathīrim
min 'ibādihi'l-mu'minīn*

"All praise be to Allah, who has preferred us over a multitude of
His believing servants."

Prophet Dawud and Prophet Suleiman ﷺ
(*al-Naml*, 27:15)

الْحَمْدُ لِلَّهِ

Al-ḥamdu li'llāh

"All praise be to Allah!"

(*al-'Ankabūt*, 29: 63)

الحَمدُ لِلَّهِ الَّذى أَذهَبَ عَنَّا الحَزَنَ ۖ إِنَّ رَبَّنا لَغفورٌ شَكورٌ

Al-ḥamdu li'llāhi'l-ladhī adhhaba 'annā'l-ḥazana innā rabbanā la-ghafūrun shakūr.

"All praise be to Allah who has forever rid us of sorrow; verily our Lord is all-forgiving, supreme in thanks."

The People of Paradise ﷺ (*Fāṭir*, 35: 34)

Part Three

Invocations of Peace and Blessings on the Prophet ﷺ

إِنَّ اللَّهَ وَمَلَائِكَتَهُ يُصَلُّونَ عَلَى النَّبِيِّ ۚ يَا أَيُّهَا الَّذِينَ آمَنُوا
صَلُّوا عَلَيْهِ وَسَلِّمُوا تَسْلِيمًا

Inna'llāha wa-malā'ikatahu yuṣallūna 'alā'l-nabī. Yā ayyuhā'l-ladhīna āmanū ṣallū 'alayhi wa-sallimū taslīmā.

"Truly Allah and His very angels ever bless the Prophet with mercy and grace: O you who believe, invoke blessings upon him, and pray your utmost he be shown all pure secure peace."

(*al-Aḥzāb*, 33: 56)

التَّحِيَّاتُ لِلَّهِ وَالصَّلَوَاتُ وَالطَّيِّبَاتُ السَّلَامُ عَلَيْكَ أَيُّهَا النَّبِيُّ
وَرَحْمَةُ اللَّهِ وَبَرَكَاتُهُ السَّلَامُ عَلَيْنَا وَعَلَى عِبَادِ اللَّهِ الصَّالِحِينَ
أَشْهَدُ أَنْ لَا إِلَهَ إِلَّا اللَّهُ وَأَشْهَدُ أَنَّ مُحَمَّدًا عَبْدُهُ وَرَسُولُهُ

Al-taḥiyyātu li'llāhi, wa'l-ṣalawātu wa'l-ṭayyibātu, al-salāmu 'alayka ayyuhā'l-nabiyyu wa-raḥmatu'llāhi wa-barakātuh, al-salāmu 'alaynā wa-'alā 'ibādi'llāhi'l-sāliḥīn. Ashhadu an lā ilāha illā Allāhu, wa-ashhadu anna Muḥammadan 'abduhu wa rasūluh.

"Greetings, blessings and the best prayers of Allah. Peace be upon you O Prophet, and the mercy of Allah and His blessings. Peace be upon us and upon Allah's righteous slaves. I testify that there is no god except Allah and that Muhammad is His slave and Messenger."

(narrated by *al-Bukhārī* and *Muslim* I/301).

اللَّهُمَّ صَلِّ عَلَى مُحَمَّدٍ وَعَلَى آلِ مُحَمَّدٍ كَمَا صَلَّيْتَ عَلَى إِبْرَاهِيمَ وَعَلَى آلِ إِبْرَاهِيمَ إِنَّكَ حَمِيدٌ مَجِيدٌ ۞ اللَّهُمَّ بَارِكْ عَلَى مُحَمَّدٍ وَعَلَى آلِ مُحَمَّدٍ كَمَا بَارَكْتَ عَلَى إِبْرَاهِيمَ وَعَلَى آلِ إِبْرَاهِيمَ إِنَّكَ حَمِيدٌ مَجِيدٌ

Allahumma ṣalli 'alā Muḥammadin wa-'alā āli Muḥammadin kamā ṣallayta 'alā Ibrāhīma wa-'ala ali Ibrāhīma, innaka ḥamīdun majīd. Allahumma bārik 'alā Muḥammadin wa-'alā āli Muḥammadin kamā bārakta 'alā Ibrāhīmā wa-'alā āli Ibrāhīma, innaka ḥamīdun majīd.

"O Allah, bless Muhammad and the folk of Muhammad as You blessed *Ibrāhīm* and the folk of *Ibrāhīm*. And show grace to Muhammad and the folk of Muhammad as You did to *Ibrāhīm* and the folk of *Ibrāhīm* in the worlds, for You are truly the Most Praiseworthy and Noble."

(narrated by *al-Bukhārī* , *Al-Asqalani, Fathul Bari*, 6/408).

اللّٰهُمَّ صَلِّ عَلى مُحَمَّدٍ وَعَلى أَزْواجِهِ وَذُرِّيَّتِهِ ۞ كَما صَلَّيْتَ عَلى آلِ إِبْراهيم. وَبارِكْ عَلى مُحَمَّدٍ وَعَلى أَزْواجِهِ وَذُرِّيَّتِهِ ۞ كَما بارَكْتَ عَلى آلِ إِبْراهيم إِنَّكَ حَميدٌ مَجيد

Allahumma ṣalli ʻalā Muḥammadin wa-ʻalā azwājihi wa-dhurriyyatihi kamā ṣallayta ʻalā āli Ibrāhim. Wa-bārik ʻalā Muḥammadin wa-ʻalā azwājihi wa-dhurriyyatihi kamā bārakta ʻalā āli Ibrāhīma, innaka ḥamīdun majīd.

"O Allah, bless Muhammad, his wives and offspring as You blessed the folk of *Ibrāhīm*. And show grace to Muhammad, his wives and offspring as You did to the folk of *Ibrāhīm*, for You are truly the Most Praiseworthy and Noble."

(narrated by *al-Bukhārī* , *Al-Asqalani, Fathul Bari*, 6/407: *Muslim*, I/306).

Part Four

The Precious Gems

The Tenets of Faith

آمَنَ الرَّسُولُ بِمَا أُنْزِلَ إِلَيْهِ مِنْ رَبِّهِ وَالْمُؤْمِنُونَ ۚ كُلٌّ آمَنَ
بِاللَّهِ وَمَلَائِكَتِهِ وَكُتُبِهِ وَرُسُلِهِ لَا نُفَرِّقُ بَيْنَ أَحَدٍ مِنْ
رُسُلِهِ ۚ وَقَالُوا سَمِعْنَا وَأَطَعْنَا ۖ غُفْرَانَكَ رَبَّنَا وَإِلَيْكَ الْمَصِيرُ

Āmana'l-rasūlu bimā unzila ilayhi min rabbihi wa'l-mu'uminūn. Kullun āmana bi'llāhi wa-malā'ikatihi wa-kutubihi wa-rusulihi lā-nufarriqu bayna aḥadin min rusulih. Wa-qālū sami'nā wa-aṭa'nā ghufrānaka Rabbanā wa-ilayka al-masīr.

"The Messenger believes in all that has been sent down to him from his Lord, as do true believers: Each and every one believes in Allah and His angels and His books and His Messengers: 'We differ not between any of His Messengers,' and all say: 'We hear, and we obey. (We seek) Your Forgiveness, our Lord, and to You is the final return.'"

Prophet Muhammad ﷺ (*al-Baqarah*, 2: 285)

لَا يُكَلِّفُ اللَّهُ نَفْسًا إِلَّا وُسْعَهَا ۚ لَهَا مَا كَسَبَتْ وَعَلَيْهَا مَا اكْتَسَبَتْ ۗ رَبَّنَا لَا تُؤَاخِذْنَا إِنْ نَسِينَا أَوْ أَخْطَأْنَا ۚ رَبَّنَا وَلَا تَحْمِلْ عَلَيْنَا إِصْرًا كَمَا حَمَلْتَهُ عَلَى الَّذِينَ مِنْ قَبْلِنَا ۚ رَبَّنَا وَلَا تُحَمِّلْنَا مَا لَا طَاقَةَ لَنَا بِهِ ۖ وَاعْفُ عَنَّا وَاغْفِرْ لَنَا وَارْحَمْنَا ۚ أَنْتَ مَوْلَانَا فَانْصُرْنَا عَلَى الْقَوْمِ الْكَافِرِينَ

Lā-yukallifu'llāhu nafsan illā wus'ahā lahā mā kasabat wa-'alayhā mā'ktasabat. Rabbanā lā tu'ākhidhnā in nasīnā aw akhṭa'nā. Rabbanā wa-lā taḥmil 'alaynā iṣran kamā ḥamaltahu 'alā'l-ladhīna min qablinā. Rabbanā wa-lā tuḥammilnā mā lā tāqata lanā bihi wa'fū 'annā wa'ighfir lanā wa'irḥamnā anta mawlānā fa'nsurnā 'alā'l-qawmi'l-kāfirīn.

"Allah does not tax any soul but with what it can bear: it shall have all it earns, and pay for what it commits. 'O Lord, take us not to task if we forget, or we make an honest mistake; O Lord, nor place upon us a binding hard burden as You did on those ever before us; nor then requite us with what we have no strength to bear; but pardon us, forgive us, and show us bounteous mercy, You are our Supreme Master, so give us triumph over the people of the unbelievers.'"

(*al-Baqarah*, 2: 286)

رَبَّنَا آمَنَّا بِمَا أَنزَلْتَ وَاتَّبَعْنَا الرَّسُولَ فَاكْتُبْنَا مَعَ الشَّاهِدِينَ

Rabbanā amannā bi-mā anzalta wa'ttaba'nā'l-rasūla fa'ktubnā ma'a'l-shāhidīn.

"Our Lord, we have believed in all You have sent down and faithfully followed the messenger, so record us among those who give witness."

Disciples of Isa (*Āl 'Imrān*, 3: 53)

قُلْ إِنَّنِي هَدَانِي رَبِّي إِلَى صِرَاطٍ مُسْتَقِيمٍ دِينًا قِيَمًا مِلَّةَ إِبْرَاهِيمَ حَنِيفًا

Qul innanī hadānī rabbī ilā ṣirāṭin mustaqīmin dīnan qiyaman millata ibrāhīma ḥanīfā.

"Say: 'I have been truly guided by my Lord to an exalted straight path: A solid upright religion: the faith given to Ibrahim, unswerving in his devotion to the primal true faith.'"

(*al-An'ām*, 6: 161)

قُلْ آمَنَّا بِاللَّهِ وَمَا أُنزِلَ عَلَيْنَا وَمَا أُنزِلَ عَلَىٰ إِبْرَاهِيمَ وَإِسْمَاعِيلَ
وَإِسْحَاقَ وَيَعْقُوبَ وَالْأَسْبَاطِ وَمَا أُوتِيَ مُوسَىٰ وَعِيسَىٰ
وَالنَّبِيُّونَ مِن رَّبِّهِمْ لَا نُفَرِّقُ بَيْنَ أَحَدٍ مِّنْهُمْ وَنَحْنُ لَهُ مُسْلِمُونَ

Qul āmannā bi'llāhi wa-mā unzila 'alaynā wa-mā unzila 'alā Ibrāhīma wa-Ismā'īla wa-Isḥāqa wa-Ya'qūba wa'l-asbāti wa-mā ūtiya Mūsā wa-'Īsā wa'l-nabiyyūna min rabbihim lā nufarriqu bayna aḥadin minhum wa-naḥnu lahu muslimūn.

"Say: 'In Allah we believe, and what has been sent down to us, and to Ibrahim, Ishmael, Ishaq, Yaqub, and the tribes, and what was given to Musa and Isa and to the prophets from their Lord: We differ between none of them, and to Him we wholly submit.'"

(*Āl 'Imrān*, 3: 84)

قُلْ إِنَّ صَلَاتِي وَنُسُكِي وَمَحْيَايَ وَمَمَاتِي لِلَّهِ رَبِّ الْعَالَمِينَ

Qul inna ṣalātī wa-nusukī wa-maḥyāya wa-mamātiya li'llāhi rabbi'l-'ālamīn.

"Say: 'Verily my prayer, my worship and sacrifice, the works of my life, and those when I die, are but for Allah, Lord of all Worlds of Beings.'"

Prophet Muhammad ﷺ (*al-An'ām* 6: 162)

وَاتَّبَعْتُ مِلَّةَ آبَآءِي إِبْرَاهِيمَ وَإِسْحَاقَ وَيَعْقُوبَ مَا كَانَ لَنَا أَن نُّشْرِكَ بِاللهِ مِن شَيْءٍ ذَٰلِكَ مِن فَضْلِ اللهِ عَلَيْنَا وَعَلَى النَّاسِ وَلَـٰكِنَّ أَكْثَرَ النَّاسِ لَا يَشْكُرُونَ

Wa'ttaba'tu millata ābā'ī Ibrāhīma wa-Isḥāqa wa-Ya'qūba mā kāna lanā an nushrika bi'llāhi min shay'in dhālika min faḍli'llāhi 'alaynā wa-'alā'l-nāsi wa-lakinna akthara'l-nāsi lā yashkurūn

"And I have wholeheartedly followed the time-honoured faith of my fathers, Ibrahim, Ishaq, and Yaqub; Nor ever was it for any of us to worship anything with Allah. That is the bounty of Allah upon us and upon mankind; but most of mankind show no thanks.'"

Prophet Yusuf ﷺ (*Yūsuf*, 12: 38)

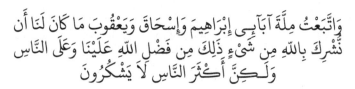

A Special Du'a For Prophet Muhammad ﷺ

قُلِ اللَّهُمَّ مَالِكَ الْمُلْكِ تُؤْتِي الْمُلْكَ مَن تَشَاء وَتَنزِعُ الْمُلْكَ مِمَّن تَشَاء وَتُعِزُّ مَن تَشَاء وَتُذِلُّ مَن تَشَاء بِيَدِكَ الْخَيْرُ إِنَّكَ عَلَى كُلِّ شَيْءٍ قَدِيرٌ

Quli'allahumma mālika'l-mulki tu'tī'l-mulka man tashā'u wa-tanzi'u'l-mulka mimman tashā'u wa-tu'izzu man tashā'u wa-tudhillu man tashā'u bi-yadika'l-khayru innaka 'alā kulli shay'in qadīr.

"Say: 'O Allah, Lord of all Sovereign Power: You give power to whomever You will, and wrest power from whomever You will; and exalt whomever You will, and abase whomever You will; in Your hand is all good; verily You have absolute power to do anything.'"

Prophet Muhammad ﷺ (*Āl 'Imrān*, 3: 26)

Seeking Protection from The Shayatin (Devils)

وقُلْ رَبِّ أَعوذُ بِكَ مِنْ هَمَزاتِ الشَّياطينِ
وَأَعوذُ بِكَ رَبِّ أَن يَحضُرون

Wa-qul rabbi a'ūdhu bika min hamazāti'l-shayāṭīni wa-a'ūdhu bika rabbi an yaḥḍurūn.

"And say: 'My Lord, I take refuge in You from the suggestions of the evil ones; and I take refuge in You, my good Lord, lest devils even come (near) me.'"

(*al-Mu'minūn*, 23: 97-98)

Seeking Protection from Black Magic, Witchcraft and the Evil Eye

Recite Sūrah al-Falaq (113: 1-5)

بِسْمِ اللَّهِ الرَّحْمَٰنِ الرَّحِيمِ

Bismi'llāhi'l-Raḥmāni'l-Raḥīm

In the name of Allah Most Merciful and Compassionate

قُلْ أَعُوذُ بِرَبِّ ٱلْفَلَقِ ۝١ مِن شَرِّ مَا خَلَقَ ۝٢ وَمِن شَرِّ غَاسِقٍ إِذَا وَقَبَ ۝٣ وَمِن شَرِّ ٱلنَّفَّٰثَٰتِ فِى ٱلْعُقَدِ ۝٤ وَمِن شَرِّ حَاسِدٍ إِذَا حَسَدَ ۝٥

Qul a'udhu bi-rabbi'l-falaq, min sharri mā khalaq, wa-min sharri ghāsiqin idhā waqab, wa-min sharri'l-naffāthāti fi'l-'uqad, wa-min sharri ḥāsidin idhā ḥasād.

"Say: I take refuge in the Lord of Daybreak, from the evil of all He has created and from the evil outpoured blackest night when it fills everything; and from the evil of wicked souls who blow spittle-mist on sorcerous knots; and from the evil of the envier when gripped by envy.'"

(*al-Falaq*, 113: 1-5)

Recite Sūrah al-Nās (114: 1-6)

بِسْمِ اللَّهِ الرَّحْمَٰنِ الرَّحِيمِ

Bismi'llāhi'l-Raḥmāni'l-Raḥīm

In the name of Allah Most Merciful and Compassionate

قُلْ أَعُوذُ بِرَبِّ ٱلنَّاسِ ﴿١﴾ مَلِكِ ٱلنَّاسِ ﴿٢﴾ إِلَٰهِ ٱلنَّاسِ ﴿٣﴾ مِن
شَرِّ ٱلْوَسْوَاسِ ٱلْخَنَّاسِ ﴿٤﴾ ٱلَّذِى يُوَسْوِسُ فِى صُدُورِ ٱلنَّاسِ ﴿٥﴾
مِنَ ٱلْجِنَّةِ وَٱلنَّاسِ ﴿٦﴾

Qul a'ūdhu bi-rabbi al-nās. Maliki al-nās. Ilāhi al-nās. Min sharri al-waswāsi al-khannās. Al-ladhī yuwaswisu fī sudūri'l-nās. Mina'l-jinnati wa'l-nās.

"Say: I take refuge in the King of Men, the God of Men; from the evil of the cunning insinuator of ill-thoughts who ever draws back from being guessed; who sows and sows ill-thoughts in breasts of men, be he of vile jinn or men.'"

(*al-Nās*, 114: 1-6)

Du'ā for the Acceptance of One's Worship ('Ibadah)

رَبَّنَا تَقَبَّلْ مِنَّا ۖ إِنَّكَ أَنْتَ السَّمِيعُ الْعَلِيمُ

Rabbanā taqabbal minnā innaka anta'l-Samī'u'l-'Alīm.

"Our Lord, accept from us; verily You are the All-hearing, the All-knowing."

Prophet Ibrahim ﷺ and Prophet Ishamel ﷺ (*al-Baqarah*, 2: 127)

Du'ā for Guidance and Assistance

بِنَصْرِ اللَّهِ يَنصُرُ مَن يَشَاء وَهُوَ الْعَزِيزُ الرَّحِيمُ

Bi-nasri'llāhi yanṣuru man yashā'u wa-huwa'l-'azīzu'l-Raḥīm.

"In the victory given by Allah: He gives victory to whomever He wills, while He is the Invincible, the All-compassionate.'"

(*al-Rūm*, 30: 5)

رَبَّنَا لاَ تُزِغْ قُلُوبَنَا بَعْدَ إِذْ هَدَيْتَنَا وَهَبْ لَنَا مِن لَّدُنكَ رَحْمَةً إِنَّكَ أَنتَ الْوَهَّابُ

Rabbanā lā tuzigh qulūbanā ba'da idh hadaytanā wa-hab lanā min ladunka raḥmatan innaka anta'l-wahhāb.

"Our Lord, turn not our hearts aside after having so completely guided us, but bestow us from Your very presence a mighty mercy, verily You alone are the Ever-bountiful Giver."

(*Āl 'Imrān*, 3: 8)

رَبَّنَا آتِنَا مِن لَّدُنكَ رَحْمَةً وَهَيِّئْ لَنَا مِنْ أَمْرِنَا رَشَدًا

Rabbanā ātinā min ladunka raḥmatan wa-hayyi' lanā min amrinā rashadā.

"Our Lord, bestow on us mercy from Yourself, and provide for us rectitude in our affairs".

(*al-Kahf*, 18: 10)

رَبِّ انصُرْنِي بِمَا كَذَّبُونِ

Rabbi'unṣurnī bi-mā kadhdhabūn.

"My Lord, come to my help at their accusation that I am lying."

Prophet Nuh (*al-Mu'minūn*, 23:26)

إِنَّ مَعِيَ رَبِّي سَيَهْدِينِ

Inna ma'iya rabbī sayahdīn.

"Verily my Lord is with me, He is sure to guide me right."

Prophet Musa (*al-Shu'arā'*, 26: 62)

Seeking Refuge from Ignorance and Wrongdoing

أَعُوذُ بِاللّهِ أَنْ أَكُونَ مِنَ الجَاهِلِينَ

A'ūdhu bi'llāhi an akūna mina'l-jāhilīn.

"I seek refuge in Allah from being of utter fools."

Prophet Musa (*al-Baqarah*, 2: 67)

رَبِّ نَجِّنِي مِنَ القَوْمِ الظَّالِمِينَ

Rabbi najjinī mina'l-qawmi'l-ẓālimīn.

"My Lord, save me from the people of wrongdoers."

Prophet Musa (*al-Qaṣaṣ*, 28: 21)

Du'ā for A Distinguished Reward

وَاجْعَل لِّي لِسَانَ صِدْقٍ فِي الْآخِرِينَ

Wa-j'al lī lisāna ṣidqin fī'l-ākhirīn.

"And grant me well-deserved and lofty praise on
every tongue of those to come."

Prophet Ibrahim (*al-Shuʻarā'*, 26: 84)

Du'ā for Rizq (Sustenance)

إِنَّ الْفَضْلَ بِيَدِ اللّهِ يُؤْتِيهِ مَن يَشَاء وَاللّهُ وَاسِعٌ عَلِيمٌ

Inna'l-faḍla bi-yadi'llāhi yu'tīhi man yashā'u wa'llāhu wāsi'un 'alīm

"Verily all favour is in the hand of Allah: He bestows it on
whomever He wills, and Allah is vast of bounty, All-Knowing."

(*Āl 'Imrān*, 3: 73)

حَسْبُنَا اللَّهُ سَيُؤْتِينَا اللَّهُ مِن فَضْلِهِ وَرَسُولُهُ إِنَّا إِلَى اللَّهِ رَاغِبُونَ

Ḥasbunā'llāhu sa-yu'tīnā Allāhu min faḍlihi wa-rasūluhu innā ilā'llāhi rāghibūn.

"Allah wholly suffices: Allah shall unfailingly give us of His vast bounty, as shall His messenger: verily from Allah alone we desire."

(*al-Tawbah*, 9: 59)

رَبِّ ٱغْفِرْ لِى وَهَبْ لِى...(*) إِنَّكَ أَنتَ ٱلْوَهَّابُ

Rabbi ghfir li wa-hab li...[*] 'innaka 'anta l-wahhab

"My Lord! Forgive me, and bestow upon me [*add your request here]... Verily, You are the Bestower."

Prophet Suleiman ﷺ (*Sad*, 38:35)

Seeking Goodness in this World and the Hereafter and Protection from the Fire

رَبَّنَا آتِنَا فِي الدُّنْيَا حَسَنَةً وَفِي الآخِرَةِ حَسَنَةً وَقِنَا عَذَابَ النَّارِ

Rabbanā ātina fi'l-Dunyā ḥasanatan wa fi'l-ākhirati ḥasanatan wa qinā 'adhāba'l-Nār.

"Our Lord, give us in this world mighty good, and in the next world mighty good, and protect us from the chastisement of the fire."

(*al-Baqarah*, 2: 201)

وَاكْتُبْ لَنَا فِي هَـذِهِ الدُّنْيَا حَسَنَةً وَفِي الآخِرَةِ إِنَّا هُدْنَـا إِلَيْكَ

Wa'ktub lanā fī hadhihi'l-dunyā ḥasanatan wa-fi'l-ākhirati innā Hūdnā ilayk.

"And inscribe for us in this short-lived world tremendous good, and in the next: Verily we repent to You in meek submission."

Prophet Musa ﷺ (*al-A'rāf*, 7: 156)

رَبِّ إِنِّي لِمَا أَنزَلْتَ إِلَيَّ مِنْ خَيْرٍ فَقِيرٌ

Rabbi innī limā anzalta ilayya min khayrin faqīr.

"My Lord, I am in utter need of any good You send me down!"

Prophet Musa (*al-Qaṣaṣ*, 28: 24)

رَبِّ ابْنِ لِي عِندَكَ بَيْتًا فِي ٱلْجَنَّةِ وَنَجِّنِي مِنَ الْقَوْمِ الظَّالِمِينَ

Rabbi ibni lī 'indaka baytan fī'l-jannati wa-najjinī
mina'l-qawmi'l-ẓālimīn.

My beloved Lord, build me an unsurpassed home with You in the luxuriant grove of Paradise, and wholly deliver me from Pharoah and all he does."

Lady Asiya, Pharoah's Wife ﷺ (*al-Taḥrīm*, 66: 11)

Du'ā to Inherit Paradise

وَاجْعَلْنِي مِن وَرَثَةِ جَنَّةِ النَّعِيمِ

Wa'j'alnī min warathati jannati'l-naʿīm.

"And make me of the heirs of the luxuriant grove of bliss."

Prophet Ibrahim (*al-Shuʿarāʾ*, 26: 85)

Seeking Protection from The Fire

رَبَّنَا مَا خَلَقْتَ هَذَا بَاطِلاً سُبْحَانَكَ فَقِنَا عَذَابَ النَّارِ

*Rabbanā mā khalaqta hadhā bāṭilan subḥānaka
faqinā ʿadhāba'l-nār.*

"Our Lord, You have not created all this in vain; You are far
above that! So keep from us the chastisement of the fire."

(*Āl ʿImrān*, 3: 191)

رَبَّنَا إِنَّكَ مَن تُدْخِلِ النَّارَ فَقَدْ أَخْزَيْتَهُ وَمَا لِلظَّالِمِينَ مِنْ أَنصَارٍ

Rabbanā innaka man tudkhili'l-nāra faqad akhzaytahu wa-mā li'-l-ẓālimīna min anṣār.

"Our Lord, verily whomever You enter the fire, You have utterly humiliated; and wrongdoers have none who can help."

(*Āl 'Imrān*, 3: 192)

رَبَّنَا اصْرِفْ عَنَّا عَذَابَ جَهَنَّمَ إِنَّ عَذَابَهَا كَانَ غَرَامًا

Rabbanā iṣrif 'annā 'adhāba jahannama inna 'adhābahā kāna gharāmā.

"Our Lord, turn from us the chastisement of the glowering hell abyss: Verily, its chastisement was ever a fearsome pursuing destruction."

(*al-Furqān*, 25: 65)

Du'ā for Light and Safety on the Day of Judgement and on the Bridge-over-Hell (al-Sirat)

رَبَّنَا أَتْمِمْ لَنَا نُورَنَا وَاغْفِرْ لَنَا إِنَّكَ عَلَى كُلِّ شَيْءٍ قَدِيرٌ

Rabbanā atmim lanā nūranā wa'ghfir lanā innaka 'alā kulli shay'in qadīr.

"Our Lord, make our light consummately entire, and forgive us; verily You have the power to do anything."

(*al-Taḥrīm*, 66: 8)

إِنَّا نَخَافُ مِن رَّبِّنَا يَوْمًا عَبُوسًا قَمْطَرِيرًا

Innā nakhāfu min rabbinā yawman 'abūsan qamṭarīrā.

"Verily, we fear from our Lord a fearsome glowering day, of ferocious terrors all wrapped up in one."

(*al-Insān*, 76: 10)

Du'ā for Wisdom and Piety

رَبِّ هَبْ لِي حُكْمًا وَأَلْحِقْنِي بِالصَّالِحِينَ

Rabbi hab lī ḥukman wa-alḥiqnī bi'l-ṣāliḥīn.

"My Lord, bestow me sovereign judgement, and perfect me in the ranks of the supremely righteous."

Prophet Ibrahim ﷺ (*al-Shu'arā'*, 26: 83)

Du'ā When Reaching the Age of Forty

حَتَّىٰٓ إِذَا بَلَغَ أَشُدَّهُۥ وَبَلَغَ أَرْبَعِينَ سَنَةً قَالَ رَبِّ أَوْزِعْنِيٓ أَنْ أَشْكُرَ نِعْمَتَكَ ٱلَّتِيٓ أَنْعَمْتَ عَلَيَّ وَعَلَىٰ وَٰلِدَيَّ وَأَنْ أَعْمَلَ صَٰلِحًا تَرْضَىٰهُ وَأَصْلِحْ لِي فِي ذُرِّيَّتِيٓ إِنِّي تُبْتُ إِلَيْكَ وَإِنِّي مِنَ ٱلْمُسْلِمِينَ

Ḥattā idhā balagha ashūddahu wa-balagha arba'īna sanatan qāla rabbi awzi'nī an ashkura ni'mataka'l-latī an'amta 'alayya wa-'alā wālidayya wa-an a'mala sāliḥan tarḍāhu wa-aṣliḥ lī fī dhurriyyatī innī tubtu ilayka wa-innī mina'l-muslimīn.

"Until, when he reaches his full manhood and its prime of forty years, he says, 'My Lord, range my whole being to show thanks for Your blessings You have bestowed on me and my parents, and to work great good to please You, and make for me all my descendents deeply righteous: Verily to You I totally repent, and am of those who to You utterly submit.'"

(*al-Aḥqāf*, 46: 15)

Du'ā to Increase in Knowledge

رَّبِّ زِدْنِي عِلْمًا

Rabbī zidnī 'ilmā.

"My Lord, increase me in knowledge."

Prophet Musa ﷺ (*Ṭa-Ha*, 20: 114)

Du'ā for Confidence and Contentment

رَبِّ اشْرَحْ لِي صَدْرِى

Rabbi ishraḥ lī Ṣādrī.

"My Lord, open wide my breast."

Prophet Musa (*Ṭa-Ha*, 20: 25)

Du'ā for Ease

وَيَسِّرْ لِي أَمْرِى

Wa-yassir lī 'amrī.

"And make easy my whole mission."

Prophet Musa (*Ṭa-Ha*, 20: 26)

Du'ā for Clarity of Speech

وَاحْلُلْ عُقْدَةً مِّن لِّسَانِي يَفْقَهُوا قَوْلِي

Wa'ḥlul 'uqdatan min lisānī yafqahū qawlī.

"And free a great knot from my tongue, and they will comprehend all I say."

Prophet Musa ﷺ (*Ṭa-Ha*, 20: 27-28)

Supplicating to Allah ﷻ to Reveal the Truth

وَيُحِقُّ اللَّهُ الحَقَّ بِكَلِماتِهِ وَلَو كَرِهَ المُجرِمونَ

Wa-yuḥiqqu'llāhu'l-ḥaqqa bi-kalimātihi wa-law kariha'l-mujrimūn.

"And Allah ever backs the Truth with His sovereign creating decrees, though committers of crimes be averse."

Prophet Musa ﷺ (*Yūnus*, 10: 82)

رَبَّنَا إِنَّكَ تَعْلَمُ مَا نُخْفِي وَمَا نُعْلِنُ وَمَا يَخْفَى عَلَى اللّهِ مِن شَيْءٍ فِي الأَرْضِ وَلاَ فِي السَّمَاء

Rabbanā innaka ta'lamu mā nukhfī wa-mā nu'linu wa-mā yakhfā 'alā'llāhi min shay'in fī'l-arḍi wa-lā fī'l-samā'.

"Our Lord, truly You know all we conceal and all we reveal; and nothing whatsoever is hidden from Allah on earth or in the sky."

(*Ibrāhīm*, 14: 38)

Seeking a Sign From Allah ﷻ

رَبِّ اجعَل لى آيَةً

Rabbi j'al li 'ayat

"O my Lord! Make a sign for me."

Prophet Zachariah ﷺ (*Āl 'Imrān*, 3:41)

Du'ā For Righteous Children

رَبِّ هَبْ لِي مِن لَّدُنكَ ذُرِّيَّةً طَيِّبَةً إِنَّكَ سَمِيعُ الدُّعَاء

Rabbi hab lī min ladunka dhurriyyatan ṭayyibatan innaka samīu'l-du'ā.

"My Lord, bestow me from You, a good offspring; verily You are the Hearer of prayers."

Prophet Zachariah (*Āl 'Imrān*, 3: 38)

فَهَبْ لِي مِن لَدُنكَ وَلِيًّا يَرِثُنِي وَيَرِثُ مِنْ آلِ يَعْقُوبَ
وَاجْعَلْهُ رَبِّ رَضِيًّا

Fa-hab lī min ladunka waliyyā yarithunī wa-yarithu min āli ya'qūba wa'j'alhu rabbi raḍiyyā.

"So bestow on me from You a son to succeed me; who will inherit all from me, and inherit something of the House of Jacob; and make him, my Lord, well-pleasing."

Prophet Zachariah (*Maryam*, 19: 5-6)

رَبِّ لَا تَذَرْنِي فَرْدًا وَأَنتَ خَيْرُ الْوَارِثِينَ

Rabbi lā tadharnī fardan wa-anta khayru'l-wārithīn.

"My Lord, leave me not destitute of any heir to carry on, and
You are the best of inheritors."

Prophet Zachariah (*al-Anbiyā'*, 21: 89)

رَبِّ هَبْ لِي مِنَ الصَّالِحِينَ

Rabbi hab lī mina'l-ṣāliḥīn.

"My Lord, bestow upon me of the truly righteous."

Prophet Ibrahim (*al-Ṣāffāt*, 37: 100)

Du'ā for Righteous Spouses and Offspring

رَبَّنَا هَبْ لَنَا مِنْ أَزْوَاجِنَا وَذُرِّيَّاتِنَا قُرَّةَ أَعْيُنٍ

Rabbanā hab lanā min azwājinā wa-dhurriyyātinā qurrata a'yun.

"Our Lord, give us from our wives and successive generations of offspring a pure joy to set eyes upon for their righteousness."

(*al-Furqān*, 25: 74)

Du'ā After Giving Birth

وَإِنِّي أُعِيذُهَا بِكَ وَذُرِّيَّتَهَا مِنَ الشَّيْطَانِ الرَّجِيمِ

Wa-'inni 'u'idhuha bika wa-dhurriyyataha mina sh-shayṭani r-rajim

"And I commend her and her offspring to Your care against (the evil of) the outcast Satan."

Hannah ﵂, wife of Imran ﵇ and the mother of Maryam ﵂
(*Āl 'Imrān*, 3: 36)

Du'ā for Guidance and Righteousness

رَبَّنَا وَاجْعَلْنَا مُسْلِمَيْنِ لَكَ وَمِن ذُرِّيَّتِنَا أُمَّةً مُّسْلِمَةً لَّكَ وَأَرِنَا مَنَاسِكَنَا وَتُبْ عَلَيْنَا إِنَّكَ أَنتَ التَّوَّابُ الرَّحِيمُ

Rabbanā waj'alnā muslimayni laka wa min dhurriyatinā ummatan muslimatan laka wa-arinā manāsikanā wa-tub 'alaynā innaka anta'l-tawwābu'l-raḥīm.

"Our Lord, make us entirely submissive to You; and make of our seed a single faith of people who wholly submit to You; and show us our rites of pilgrimage, and forgive us all: verily You are the Oft-forgiving, the All-Compassionate."

Prophet Ibrahim ﷺ (*al-Baqarah*, 2: 128)

رَبِّ إِنَّ ابْنِي مِنْ أَهْلِي وَإِنَّ وَعْدَكَ الْحَقُّ وَأَنتَ أَحْكَمُ الْحَاكِمِينَ

Rabbi inna ibnī min ahlī wa-inna wa'daka al-ḥaqqu wa-anta aḥkamu'l-ḥakimin.

"My Lord, verily my son is of my family, and Your promise is true; and You are the Most Just of judges."

Prophet Nuh ﷺ (*Hūd*, 11: 45)

فاطِرَ السَّماواتِ وَالأَرضِ أَنتَ وَلِيّي فِي الدُّنيا وَالآخِرَةِ ۖ تَوَفَّني مُسلِمًا وَأَلحِقني بِالصّالِحينَ

Fātira'l-samāwāti wa'l-arḍi anta waliyyi fi'l-dunyā wa'l-ākhirati tawaffanī musliman wa-alḥiqnī bi'l-sāliḥīn.

"Originator of the Heavens and Earth: You are my Ever-Powerful Friend and Protector in this world and the next; take back my soul in whole submission to You as a Muslim, and put me among the supremely righteous."

Prophet Yusuf ﷺ (*Yūsuf*, 12: 101)

رَبِّ اجْعَلْنِي مُقِيمَ الصَّلاَةِ ومِن ذُرِّيَّتِي رَبَّنَا وَتَقَبَّلْ دُعَاء

Rabbi ij'alnī muqīma al-salāti wa-min dhurriyyatī rabbanā wa-taqabbal du'ā'.

"My Lord, make me keep well the prayer, and of my offspring, our Lord; and graciously accept my plea."

Prophet Ibrahim ﷺ (*Ibrāhīm*, 14: 40)

Du'ā For Parents

رَبَّنَا اغْفِرْ لِي وَلِوَالِدَيَّ وَلِلْمُؤْمِنِينَ يَوْمَ يَقُومُ الْحِسَابُ

*Rabbanā ighfir lī wa-li-wālidayya wa-li'l-mu'minīna yawma
yaqūmu'l-ḥisāb.*

"Our Lord, forgive me and my parents, and all believers, on the
day the Reckoning shall stand."

Prophet Ibrahim (*Ibrāhīm*, 14: 41)

رَّبِّ ارْحَمْهُمَا كَمَا رَبَّيَانِي صَغِيرًا

Rabbi irḥamhumā kamā rabbayānī saghīrā.

"My Lord, show them mercy, the way they raised
me when I was a child."

(*al-Isrā'*, 17: 24)

وَٱغْفِرْ لِأَبِىٓ إِنَّهُۥ كَانَ مِنَ ٱلضَّآلِّينَ

Waghfir li-'abi 'innahu kana mina ẓāliīn.

"And forgive my father, verily he is of the erring."

Prophet Ibrahim ﷺ (*al-Shu'arā'*, 26:86)

Du'ā in Times of Trial

رَبِّ لَوْ شِئْتَ أَهْلَكْتَهُم مِّن قَبْلُ وَإِيَّاىَ أَتُهْلِكُنَا بِمَا فَعَلَ السُّفَهَاء مِنَّا إِنْ هِىَ إِلاَّ فِتْنَتُكَ تُضِلُّ بِهَا مَن تَشَاء وَتَهْدِى مَن تَشَاء أَنتَ وَلِيُّنَا فَاغْفِرْ لَنَا وَارْحَمْنَا وَأَنتَ خَيْرُ الْغَافِرِينَ

Rabbi law shi'ta ahlaktahum min qablu wa-iyyāya atuhlikunā bimā fa'ala'l-sufahā'u minnā in hiya illā fitnatuka tuḍillu bihā man tashā'u wa-tahdī man tashā'u anta waliyyunā fa'ghfir lanā wa'rḥamnā wa-anta khayru'l-ghāfirīn.

"My Lord, had You wished, You could have destroyed them at any time before and me alike; would You destroy us for what the fools of us have done? It is naught but Your dire trial of us: You misguide by it whomever You will: You are our All-Protecting Friend and Guardian, so forgive us and show us mercy, and you are the best of any who forgive."

Prophet Musa ﷺ (*al-A'rāf*, 7: 155)

ٱلَّذِينَ ءَامَنُوا مَعَهُۥ مَتَىٰ نَصْرُ ٱللَّهِ ۗ أَلَآ إِنَّ نَصْرَ ٱللَّهِ قَرِيبٌ

al-ladhina 'amanu ma'ahu mata naṣru-Allahi,
'Ala inna naṣraAllahi Qarib.

"When (will come) the Help of Allah?" Yes! Certainly, the Help of Allah is near!"

(*al-Baqarah*, 2: 214)

Duʿā When Afflicted with a Calamity

إِنَّا لِلَّهِ وَإِنَّـا إِلَيْهِ رَاجِعونَ

Innā li'llāhi wa-innā ilayhi rājiʿūn.

"Verily we are Allah's, and to Him are we bound to return."

(*al-Baqarah*, 2: 156)

لَا تَحْزَنْ إِنَّ اللَّهَ مَعَنا

Lā taḥzan inna'llāha ma'anā.

"Grieve not, Allah is truly with us."

(*al-Tawbah*, 9: 40)

Du'ā when in Distress and Pain

أَنِّي مَسَّنِيَ الضُّرُّ وَأَنتَ أَرْحَمُ الرَّاحِمِينَ

Annī massaniya'l-ḍurru wa-anta arḥamu'l-rāḥimīn.

"Verily, affliction has touched me, and You are the Most
Merciful of the Merciful."

Prophet Ayoub (*al-Anbiyā'*, 21: 83)

Seeking Help when Overburdened

لَا يُكَلِّفُ ٱللَّهُ نَفْسًا إِلَّا وُسْعَهَا ۚ لَهَا مَا كَسَبَتْ وَعَلَيْهَا مَا
ٱكْتَسَبَتْ رَبَّنَا لَا تُؤَاخِذْنَآ إِن نَّسِينَآ أَوْ أَخْطَأْنَا ۚ رَبَّنَا وَلَا
تَحْمِلْ عَلَيْنَآ إِصْرًا كَمَا حَمَلْتَهُۥ عَلَى ٱلَّذِينَ مِن قَبْلِنَا ۚ رَبَّنَا وَلَا
تُحَمِّلْنَا مَا لَا طَاقَةَ لَنَا بِهِۦ ۖ وَٱعْفُ عَنَّا وَٱغْفِرْ لَنَا وَٱرْحَمْنَآ
أَنتَ مَوْلَىٰنَا فَٱنصُرْنَا عَلَى ٱلْقَوْمِ ٱلْكَٰفِرِينَ

Lā yukallifu'llāhu nafsan illā wus'ahā lahā mā kasabat wa-'alayhā mā'ktasabat. Rabbanā lā tu'ākhidhnā in nasīnā aw akhṭa'nā. Rabbanā wa-lā taḥmil 'alaynā iṣran kamā ḥamaltahu 'alā'l-ladhīna min qablinā. Rabbanā wa-lā tuḥammilnā mā lā ṭāqata lanā bihi wa'fu annā wa'ghfir lanā wa'rḥamnā anta mawlānā fa'nṣurnā 'alā'l-qawmi'l-kāfirīn.

"O Lord, take us not to task if we forget, or make an honest mistake; O Lord, nor place upon us a binding hard burden as You did on those ever before us; nor then requite us with what we have no strength to bear; but pardon us, forgive us, and show us bounteous mercy, You are our Supreme Master, so give us triumph over the people of the unbelievers."

(*al-Baqarah*, 2: 286)

لَّا إِلَهَ إِلَّا أَنتَ سُبْحَانَكَ إِنِّي كُنتُ مِنَ الظَّالِمِينَ

Lā ilāha illā anta subḥānaka innī kuntu mina'l-ẓālimīn.

"No god is there but You; gloriously exalted are You above all;
verily was I of the utter wrongdoers."

Prophet Yunus (*al-Anbiyā'*, 21: 87)

أَنِّي مَغْلُوبٌ فَانتَصِرْ

Annī maghlūbun fa'ntaṣir.

"Verily I am overcome: so be my help!"

Prophet Nuh (*al-Qamar*, 54: 10)

Seeking Protection from Oppressors

رَبَّنَا أَخْرِجْنَا مِنْ هَـٰذِهِ الْقَرْيَةِ الظَّالِمِ أَهْلُهَا وَاجْعَل لَّنَا مِن لَّدُنكَ وَلِيًّا وَاجْعَل لَّنَا مِن لَّدُنكَ نَصِيرًا

Rabbanā akhrijnā min hadhihi'l-qaryati'l-ẓālimi ahluhā wa'j'al lanā min ladunka waliyyan wa'j'al lanā min ladunka nasīrā.

"Our Lord, take us out of this town whose people are idolatrous oppressors, and bestow us from Yourself a powerful protector, and bestow us from Yourself a powerful ally."

(*al-Nisā'*, 4: 75)

وَنَجِّنَا بِرَحْمَتِكَ مِنَ الْقَوْمِ الْكَافِرِينَ

Wa-najjinā bi-raḥmatika mina'l-qawmi al-kāfirīn.

"And deliver us by Your mercy from the people of the unbelievers."

(*Yūnus*, 10: 86)

رَبِّ نَجِّنِي وَأَهْلِي مِمَّا يَعْمَلُونَ

Rabbi najjinī wa-ahlī mimmā yaʿmalūn.

"My Lord, deliver me and my household from
the blight of their deed!"

Prophet Lut (*al-Shuʿarāʾ* 26: 169)

رَبِّ انصُرْنِي عَلَى الْقَوْمِ الْمُفْسِدِينَ

Rabbi inṣurnī ʿalā'l-qawmi'l-mufsidīn.

"My Lord, give me final triumph over the people
who work corruption."

Prophet Lut (*al-ʿAnkabūt*, 29: 30)

To Avoid Confrontation for the Sake of Allah

وَإِن كَذَّبُوكَ فَقُل: لِّي عَمَلِي وَلَكُمْ عَمَلُكُمْ أَنتُمْ بَرِيئُونَ
مِمَّا أَعْمَلُ وَأَنَا۠ بَرِىٓءٌ مِّمَّا تَعْمَلُونَ

Wa-in kadhdhabūka fa-qul: Lī 'amalī wa-lakum 'amalukum antum barī'ūna mimmā a'malu wa-anā barī'un mimmā ta'malūn.

"And should they stubbornly cry you lies. Say: 'I have my deeds, and you have yours. You are innocent of what I do, and I am innocent of what you do.'"

(*Yūnus*, 10: 41)

Special Protection (Being Veiled by Allah)

وَإِذَا قَرَأْتَ ٱلْقُرْءَانَ جَعَلْنَا بَيْنَكَ وَبَيْنَ ٱلَّذِينَ لَا يُؤْمِنُونَ
بِٱلْـَٔاخِرَةِ حِجَابًا مَّسْتُورًا

Wa-idhā qara ta l-qur āna ja alnā baynaka wa-bayna lladhīna lā yu minūna bi-l-ākhirati ḥijāban mastūra

"When you recite the Qurān, We draw between you and those who do not believe in the Hereafter, an invisible veil."

(*Al-Isra*, 17:45)

To Overcome an Oppressor; Oppressive Ruler and Seeking Patience

رَبَّنَا أَفْرِغْ عَلَيْنَا صَبْرًا وَثَبِّتْ أَقْدَامَنَا وَانصُرْنَا عَلَى الْقَوْمِ الْكَافِرِينَ

*Rabbanā afrigh 'alaynā ṣabran wa-thabbit aqdāmanā wa'nṣurnā
'alā'l-qawmi'l-kāfirīn.*

"Our Lord! Pour forth on us patience, set our feet firm and make
us victorious over the disbelieving people."

King Talut ◆ (al-Baqarah, 2: 250)

رَبَّنَا اطْمِسْ عَلَىٰ أَمْوَالِهِمْ وَاشْدُدْ عَلَىٰ قُلُوبِهِمْ فَلَا يُؤْمِنُوا حَتَّىٰ
يَرَوُا الْعَذَابَ الْأَلِيمَ

*Rabbanā'iṭmis 'alā amwālihim wa'shdud 'alā qulūbihim fa-lā
yu'minū ḥattā yarawū'l-'adhāba'l-alīm.*

"Our Lord, wipe out all trace of their wealth, and seize fast upon
their hearts so they believe not, until they behold the painful
chastisement."

Prophet Musa ◆ (*Yūnus*, 10: 88)

رَبَّنَا إِنَّنَا نَخَافُ أَن يَفْرُطَ عَلَيْنَا أَوْ أَن يَطْغَى

Rabbanā innanā nakhāfu an yafruṭa 'alaynā aw an yaṭghā.

"Our Lord, verily we fear he may commit excess against us, or transgress all limits."

Prophet Musa and Prophet Haroun ☙ (*Ṭa-Ha*, 20: 45)

Du'ā for Justice

رَبِّ احْكُم بِالْحَقِّ وَرَبُّنَا الرَّحْمَٰنُ الْمُسْتَعَانُ عَلَى مَا تَصِفُونَ

Rabbi iḥkum bi'l-ḥaqqi wa-rabbunā'l-raḥmānu'l-musta'ānu 'alā mā taṣifūn.

"My Lord, decide between us in complete truth; And our Lord is the All-Merciful who alone avails against what you describe."

Prophet Muhammad ☙ (*al-Anbiyā'*, 21: 112)

Du‘ā: Allah ﷻ Never Breaks His Promise

رَبَّنَا إِنَّكَ جَامِعُ النَّاسِ لِيَوْمٍ لاَّ رَيْبَ فِيهِ إِنَّ اللّهَ لاَ يُخْلِفُ الْمِيعَادَ

Rabbanā innaka jāmi‘u’l-nāsi li-yawmin lā rayba fīhi inna’llāha lā yukhlifu’l-mī‘ād.

“Our Lord, truly You shall amass mankind for an unspeakable day, no doubt is there in it; verily Allah never breaks His promise”.

(*Āl ‘Imrān*, 3: 9)

رَبَّنَا وَآتِنَا مَا وَعَدتَّنَا عَلَى رُسُلِكَ وَلاَ تُخْزِنَا يَوْمَ الْقِيَامَةِ إِنَّكَ لاَ تُخْلِفُ الْمِيعَادَ

Rabbanā wa-ātinā mā wa‘adtanā ‘alā rusulika wa-lā tukhzinā yawma’l-qiyāmati innaka lā tukhlifu’l-mī‘ād

“Our Lord, and bestow us what You have promised us on the tongues of Your Messengers; nor humiliate us on the Day of Resurrection; verily You never break Your word.”

(*Āl ‘Imrān*, 3: 194)

Trust in and Reliance on Allah ﷻ

إِن يَنصُرْكُمُ اللَّهُ فَلَا غَالِبَ لَكُمْ وَإِن يَخْذُلْكُمْ فَمَن ذَا الَّذِي يَنصُرُكُم مِّن بَعْدِهِ وَعَلَى اللَّهِ فَلْيَتَوَكَّلِ الْمُؤْمِنُونَ

In yansurkumu'llāhu fa-lā ghāliba lakum wa-'in yakhdhulkum fa-man dhā' l-ladhī yanṣurukum min ba'dihi wa-'ala'llahi fa'-l-yatawakkali' l-mu'minūn.

"If Allah gives you triumph, none may defeat you; and if He forsakes you, who should help you after Him? And in Allah let believers put their trust."

(*Āl 'Imrān*, 3: 160)

وَشَاوِرْهُمْ فِي الْأَمْرِ فَإِذَا عَزَمْتَ فَتَوَكَّلْ عَلَى اللَّهِ إِنَّ اللَّهَ يُحِبُّ الْمُتَوَكِّلِينَ

Wa-shāwirhum fi'l-amri fa-idhā 'azamta fa-tawakkal 'alā'llāhi inna'llāha yuḥibbu'l-mutawakkilīn

"... and consult with them on matters of importance; and when you decide, then trust wholly to Allah: verily Allah loves those who trust in Him."

(*Āl 'Imrān*, 3: 159)

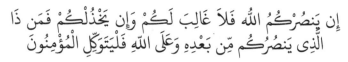

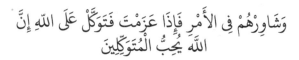

إِلَّآ أَن يَشَاءَ اللَّهُ رَبُّنَا وَسِعَ رَبُّنَا كُلَّ شَيْءٍ عِلْمًا عَلَى اللَّهِ تَوَكَّلْنَا رَبَّنَا افْتَحْ بَيْنَنَا وَبَيْنَ قَوْمِنَا بِالْحَقِّ وَأَنتَ خَيْرُ الْفَاتِحِينَ

Illā an yashā'a'llāhu rabbunā wasi'a rabbunā kulla shay'in 'ilman 'ala'llāhi tawakkalnā Rabbanā'ftaḥ baynanā wa-bayna qawminā bi'l-ḥaqqi wa-anta khayru'l-fātiḥīn.

"... save only if Allah our Lord wills; our Lord encompasses everything in knowledge; in Allah alone we trust. Our Lord, judge between us and our people, with whole truth; and You are the best of judges."

(*al-A'rāf*, 7: 89)

لَّن يُصِيبَنَا إِلَّآ مَا كَتَبَ اللَّهُ لَنَا هُوَ مَوْلَانَا

Lan yuṣībanā illā ma kataba'llāhu lanā huwa mawlānā.

"Nothing shall strike us but what Allah has inscribed in our favour: He is our Supreme Master."

(*al-Tawbah*, 9: 51)

حَسْبُنَا اللَّهُ سَيُؤْتِينَا اللَّهُ مِن فَضْلِهِ وَرَسُولُهُ إِنَّا إِلَى اللَّهِ رَاغِبُونَ

Ḥasbunā'llāhu sa-yu'tīnā Allāhu min faḍlihi wa-rasūluhu innā ilā'llāhi rāghibūn.

"Allah wholly suffices: Allah shall unfailingly give us of His vast bounty, as shall His Messenger: verily from Allah alone we desire."

(*al-Tawbah*, 9: 59)

حَسْبِيَ اللَّهُ لا إِلَـهَ إِلاَّ هُوَ عَلَيْهِ تَوَكَّلْتُ وَهُوَ رَبُّ الْعَرْشِ الْعَظِيمِ

Ḥasbiya'llāhu lā ilāha illā huwa 'alayhi tawakkaltu wa-huwa rabbu'l-'arshi'l-'aẓīm.

"Allah is sufficient for me; there is no god but He; in Him I put my trust, and He is Lord of the Mighty Throne."

(*al-Tawbah*, 9: 129)

إِنِّي تَوَكَّلْتُ عَلَى اللهِ رَبِّي وَرَبِّكُم مَّا مِن دَآبَّةٍ إِلاَّ هُوَ آخِذٌ بِنَاصِيَتِهَا إِنَّ رَبِّي عَلَى صِرَاطٍ مُّسْتَقِيمٍ

Innī tawakkaltu 'alā'llāhi rabbī wa-rabbikum mā min dābbatin illā huwa ākhidhun bi-nāsiyatihā inna rabbī 'alā sirātin mustaqīm.

"Verily I put my whole trust in Allah, my Lord and your Lord: there is no creature, but He holds it fast by its devising forehead: verily my Lord is upon an exalted straight way."

Prophet Hud (*Hūd*, 11: 56)

إِنِ الْحُكْمُ إِلاَّ لِلّهِ عَلَيْهِ تَوَكَّلْتُ وَعَلَيْهِ فَلْيَتَوَكَّلِ الْمُتَوَكِّلُونَ

Ini al-ḥukmu illā li'llāhi 'alayhi tawakkaltu wa-'alayhi fa'l-yatawakkali'l-mutawakkilūn.

"Decision is Allah's alone; on Him do I rely; so in Him let all who would rely place their trust."

Prophet Ya'qub (*Yūsuf*, 12: 67)

هُوَ رَبِّي لا إِلَـهَ إِلاَّ هُوَ عَلَيْهِ تَوَكَّلْتُ وَإِلَيْهِ مَتَابِ

Huwa rabbī lā ilāha illā huwa 'alayhi tawakkaltu wa-ilayhi matāb.

"He is my Lord, no god is there but He; in Him I put my trust, and to Him is my utter repentance."

(*al-Ra'd*, 13: 30)

حَسْبِيَ اللَّهُ عَلَيْهِ يَتَوَكَّلُ الْمُتَوَكِّلُونَ

Ḥasbiya'llāhu 'alayhi yatawakkalu'l-mutawakkilūn.

"Allah suffices me; in Him do those who rely put their trust."

(*al-Zumar*, 39: 38)

رَبَّنَا عَلَيْكَ تَوَكَّلْنَا وَإِلَيْكَ أَنَبْنَا وَإِلَيْكَ الْمَصِيرُ

Rabbanā 'alayka tawakkalnā wa-ilayka anabnā wa-ilayka'l-masīr.

"Our Lord, on You do we rely, to You do we ever return from error in love and devotion, and to You is the final end."

Prophet Ibrahim ﷺ (*al-Mumtaḥanah*, 60: 4)

هُوَ الرَّحْمَٰنُ آمَنَّا بِهِ وَعَلَيْهِ تَوَكَّلْنَا

Huwa'l-raḥmānu āmannā bihi wa-'alayhi tawakkalnā.

"He is the All-Merciful; we believe in Him; and in Him we trust."

(*al-Mulk*, 67: 29)

Du'ā when on a Journey

رَّبِّ أَنزِلْنِي مُنزَلًا مُّبَارَكًا وَأَنتَ خَيْرُ الْمُنزِلِينَ

Rabbi anzilnī munzalan mubārakan wa-anta khayru'l-munzilīn.

"My Lord, bring me to a landfall forever blessed, while You are the best who give place to dwell."

Prophet Nuh ﷺ (*al-Mu'minūn*, 23: 29)

سُبْحانَ الَّذِى سَخَّرَ لَنَا هَذَا وَمَا كُنَّا لَهُ مُقْرِنِينَ

Subḥāna'l-ladhī sakhkhara lanā hadhā wa-mā kunnā lahu muqrinīn.

"Exalted in limitless glory is He who made even this tamely submissive to us; while never could we have brought it to rein."

(*al-Zukhruf*, 43: 13)

وَإِنَّا إِلَى رَبِّنَا لَمُنقَلِبُونَ

Wa-'innā 'ilā rabbinā la-munqalibūn.

"And verily to our Lord we are returning home."

(*al-Zukhruf*, 43: 14)

Asking for Security for One's Land and Guidance for One's Children

رَبِّ اجْعَلْ هَـٰذَا الْبَلَدَ آمِنًا وَاجْنُبْنِي وَبَنِيَّ أَن نَّعْبُدَ الْأَصْنَامَ

Rabbi ij'al hadha'l-balada āminan wa'jnubnī wa-baniyya an na'buda'l-asnām.

"My Lord, make this township wholly secure, and make me and my sons and theirs shun worshipping idols."

Prophet Ibrahim (*Ibrāhīm*, 14: 35)

Asking for Security for One's Land and for Sustenance

رَبِّ اجْعَل هٰذا بَلَدًا آمِنًا وَارزُقْ أَهلَهُ مِنَ الثَّمَرَاتِ مَن آمَنَ
مِنهُم بِاللَّهِ وَاليَومِ الآخِرِ

Rabbi ij'al hadha baladan āminan wa'rzuq ahlahu mina'l-thamarāti man āmana minhum bi'llāhi wa'l-yawmi'l-ākhir.

"My Lord, make this township wholly secure, and ever provide for its folk of the fruits of fertile crops, those of them who believe in Allah and the Last Day."

Prophet Ibrahim (*al-Baqarah*, 2: 126)

Du'ā for Constant Glorification, Gratitude and Remembrance of Allah ﷻ

كَيْ نُسَبِّحَكَ كَثِيراً

Kay nusabbiḥaka kathīrā.

"That we may proclaim to all Your incomparable glory above that they utter."

Prophet Musa ﷺ (*Ṭa-Ha*, 20: 33)

الحَمدُ لِلَّهِ الَّذى نَجّانا مِنَ القَومِ الظّالِمينَ

Al-ḥamdu li'llāhi'l-ladhī najjānā mina'l-qawmi'l-ẓālimīn.

"All praise is Allah's who has truly delivered us from the people of the godless (wrongdoers)."

Prophet Nuh ﷺ (*al-Mu'minūn*, 23: 28)

الْحَمْدُ لِلّٰهِ الَّذِى فَضَّلَنَا عَلَى كَثِيرٍ مِّنْ عِبَادِهِ الْمُؤْمِنِينَ

Al-ḥamdu li'llāhi'l-ladhī faḍalanā 'alā kathīrim
min 'ibādihi'l-mu'minīn.

"All praise be to Allah , who has preferred us over a multitude
of His believing servants."

Prophet Dawud and Prophet Suleiman ﷺ (*al-Naml*, 27: 15)

❖〈◆◇◆〉❖

رَبِّ بِمَا أَنْعَمْتَ عَلَيَّ فَلَنْ أَكُونَ ظَهِيرًا لِّلْمُجْرِمِينَ

Rabbi bimā an'amta 'alayya fa-lan akūna zahīran li'l-mujrimīn.

"My Lord, for Your blessing me, nevermore shall I aid the
committers of crimes."

Prophet Musa ﷺ (*al-Qaṣaṣ*, 28: 17)

Du'ā when Thanking Allah ﷻ

قَدْ أَنْعَمَ اللَّهُ عَلَيَّ إِذْ لَمْ أَكُن مَّعَهُمْ شَهِيدًا

Qad an'ama'llāhu 'alayya idh lam akun ma'ahum shahīdā.

"Allah truly blessed me , as I was not there with them."

(*al-Nisā'*, 4: 72)

الحَمدُ لِلَّهِ الَّذى وَهَبَ لى ... إِنَّ رَبِّى لَسَميعُ الدُّعاءِ

Al-ḥamdu li'llāhi'l-ladhī wahaba lī ...[*] inna rabbī la-samī'u'l-du'ā'.

"All praise be to Allah who has bestowed me ... [*mention the blessing here] . . . Verily, my Lord is the Hearer of prayers."

Prophet Ibrahim ﷺ (*Ibrāhīm*, 14: 39)

وَنَذْكُرَكَ كَثِيراً

Wa-nadhkuraka kathīrā

"And remember You much."

Prophet Musa (*Ṭa-Ha*, 20:34)

رَبِّ أَوْزِعْنِي أَنْ أَشْكُرَ نِعْمَتَكَ الَّتِي أَنْعَمْتَ عَلَيَّ وَعَلَى
وَالِدَيَّ وَأَنْ أَعْمَلَ صَالِحًا تَرْضَاهُ وَأَدْخِلْنِي بِرَحْمَتِكَ فِي
عِبَادِكَ الصَّالِحِينَ

*Rabbi awzi'nī an ashkura ni'mataka'l-latī an'amta 'alayya wa-
'alā wālidayya wa-an a'mala sāliḥan tarḍāhu wa-adkhilnī bi-
raḥmatika fī 'ibādika'l-sāliḥīn.*

"My Lord, range my whole being to show thanks for Your
blessings You have endowed me and my parents with, and I do
righteous work that You find pleasing; and enter me by Your
mercy into the eternal company of Your righteous servants."

Prophet Suleiman (*al-Naml*, 27: 19)

الحَمدُ لِلَّهِ الَّذى نَجّانا مِنَ القَومِ الظّالِمينَ

Al-ḥamdu li'llāhi'l-ladhī najjāna mina'l-qawmi'l-ẓālimīn.

"All praise is Allah's, who has truly delivered us from the people of the godless."

Prophet Nuh (*al-Mu'minūn*, 23: 28)

Part Five

Invocations for Forgiveness

Seeking Allah's Forgiveness

غُفْرَانَكَ رَبَّنَا وَإِلَيْكَ الْمَصِيرُ

Ghufrānaka Rabbanā wa ilayka'l-masīr.

"(We seek) Your own divine forgiveness, our Lord, and to You is the final return."

(*al-Baqarah*, 2: 285)

رَبَّنَا إِنَّنَا آمَنَّا فَاغْفِرْ لَنَا ذُنُوبَنَا وَقِنَا عَذَابَ النَّارِ

Rabbanā innanā āmannā fa'ghfir lanā dhunūbanā wa-qinā 'adhāba'l-nār.

"Our Lord, verily we have believed, so forgive us our sins, and keep us from the chastisement of the fire."

(*Āl 'Imrān*, 3: 16)

رَبَّنَا فَاغْفِرْ لَنَا ذُنُوبَنَا

Rabbanā fa'ghfir lanā dhunūbanā.

"Our Lord, so forgive us our sins."

(*Āl 'Imrān*, 3: 193)

رَبَّنَا ظَلَمْنَا أَنفُسَنَا وَإِن لَّمْ تَغْفِرْ لَنَا وَتَرْحَمْنَا لَنَكُونَنَّ مِنَ الْخَاسِرِينَ

Rabbanā ẓalamnā anfusanā wa-in lam taghfir lanā wa-tarḥamnā la-nakūnanna mina'l-khāsirīn.

"Our Lord, we have wronged ourselves, and if You do not forgive us and show us mercy, we shall be of the wholly ruined."

(*al-A'rāf*, 7: 23)

هُوَ رَبِّي لَا إِلَٰهَ إِلَّا هُوَ عَلَيْهِ تَوَكَّلْتُ وَإِلَيْهِ مَتَابِ

Huwa rabbī lā ilāha illā huwa 'alayhi tawakkaltu wa-ilayhi matāb.

"He is my Lord; no god is there but He; in Him I put my trust, and to Him is my return with utter repentance."

(*al-Ra'd*, 13: 30)

رَبَّنَا آمَنَّا فَاغْفِرْ لَنَا وَارْحَمْنَا وَأَنتَ خَيْرُ الرَّاحِمِينَ

Rabbanā āmannā fa'ghfir lanā wa'rḥamnā wa-anta khayru'l-rāḥimīn.

"Our Lord, we have believed: so forgive us our wrongs, and bestow us the bounties of Your mercy, and You are the best of the merciful."

(*al-Mu'minūn*, 23: 109)

رَبَّنَا اغْفِرْ لَنَا وَلِإِخْوَانِنَا الَّذِينَ سَبَقُونَا بِالْإِيمَانِ

Rabbanā ighfir lanā wa-li-ikhwāninā'l-ladhīna Sabaqūna bi'l-īmān.

"Our Lord, forgive us and our brethren who won unto true faith before us."

(*al-Ḥashr*, 59: 10)

Repentance of the Prophets

Prophet Adam and Lady Hawwa

رَبَّنَا ظَلَمْنَا أَنْفُسَنَا وَإِنْ لَمْ تَغْفِرْ لَنَا وَتَرْحَمْنَا لَنَكُونَنَّ مِنَ الْخَاسِرِينَ

Rabbanā ẓalamnā anfusanā wa-in lam taghfir lanā wa-tarḥamnā la-nakūnanna mina'l-khāsirīn.

"Our Lord, we have wronged ourselves, and if You do not forgive us and show us mercy, we shall be of the wholly ruined."

(al-Aʻrāf, 7: 23)

Prophet Nūḥ

رَبِّ اغْفِرْ لِي وَلِوَالِدَيَّ وَلِمَن دَخَلَ بَيْتِيَ مُؤْمِنًا وَلِلْمُؤْمِنِينَ وَالْمُؤْمِنَاتِ

Rabbi ighfir lī wa-li-wālidayya wa-li-man dakhala baytiya mu'minan wa-li'l-mu'minīna wa'l-mu'mināt.

"My Lord, forgive me and my parents, and everyone who has entered my home a believer, and men and women who truly believe."

(Nūḥ, 71:28)

Prophet Ibrāhīm ﷺ

وَتُبۡ عَلَيۡنَآۖ إِنَّكَ أَنتَ ٱلتَّوَّابُ ٱلرَّحِيمُ

Wa-tub ʿalaynā innaka antaʾl-tawwabuʾl-raḥīm.

"And accept our repentance; truly, You are the oft-forgiving, the All-compassionate."

(*al-Baqarah*, 2: 128)

رَّبَّنَا عَلَيۡكَ تَوَكَّلۡنَا وَإِلَيۡكَ أَنَبۡنَا وَإِلَيۡكَ ٱلۡمَصِيرُ

Rabbanā ʿalayka tawakkalnā wa-ilayka anabnā wa-ilaykaʾl-maṣīr

"Our Lord, on You do we rely, to You do we ever return from error in love and devotion, and to You is the final return."

(*al-Mumtaḥanah*, 60: 4)

Prophet Musa

سُبحانَكَ تُبتُ إِلَيَكَ

Subḥānaka tubtu ilayk.

"Glory be to you; to You I turn in repentence."

(al-Aʿrāf, 7: 143)

رَبِّ اغْفِرْ لِي وَلِأَخِي وَأَدْخِلْنَا فِي رَحْمَتِكَ وَأَنتَ أَرْحَمُ الرَّاحِمِينَ

Rabbi ighfir lī wa-li-akhī wa-adkhilnā fī raḥmatika wa-anta arḥamu'l-rahimin.

"O my Lord, forgive me and my brother and enter us into Your mercy and You are the most Merciful."

(Al-Aʿrāf, 7: 151)

أَنتَ وَلِيُّنا فَاغفِر لَنا وَارحَمنا ۖ وَأَنتَ خَيرُ الغافِرينَ

Anta waliyyunā fa'ghfir lanā wa'rḥamnā wa-anta khayru'l-ghāfirīn.

"You are our All-Protecting Friend and Guardian, so forgive us and show us mercy, and You are the best of those who forgive."

(*al-A'rāf*, 7: 155)

رَبِّ إِنّى ظَلَمتُ نَفسى فَاغفِر لى فَغَفَرَ لَهُ ۚ إِنَّهُ هُوَ الغَفورُ الرَّحيمُ

Rabbi innī ẓalamtu nafsī fa'ghfir lī fa-ghafara lahu innahu huwa'l-ghafūru'l-raḥīm.

"'My Lord, truly I have wronged myself, so forgive me'; So He forgave him; verily He alone is the All-Forgiving."

(*al- Qaṣaṣ*, 28: 16)

Prophet Suleiman

رَبِّ اغْفِرْ لِي

Rabbi ighfir lī.

"My Lord, forgive me."

(*Sād*, 38: 35)

Queen Sheba

رَبِّ إِنِّي ظَلَمتُ نَفسى

Rabbi innī ẓalamtu nafsī.

"My Lord, verily I have been idolatrously wronging my own soul."

(*al-Naml*, 27: 44)

Prophet Yūnus

لَا إِلَهَ إِلَّا أَنْتَ سُبْحَانَكَ إِنِّي كُنْتُ مِنَ الظَّالِمِينَ

Lā ilāha illā anta subḥānaka innī kuntu mina'l-ẓālimīn.

"No god is there but You; gloriously exalted are You above all;
verily was I of the utter wrongdoers."

(*al-Anbiyā'*, 21: 86)

Prophet Muhammad

رَّبِّ اغْفِرْ وَارْحَمْ وَأَنتَ خَيْرُ الرَّاحِمِينَ

Rabbi ighfir wa'rḥam wa-anta khayru'l-rāḥimīn.

"My Lord, forgive us our wrongs, and bestow us the bounties of
Your mercy, and You are the best of the merciful."

(*al-Mu'minūn* 23: 118)

A Concluding Prayer

Bismi Allāhi al-Raḥmāni al-Raḥīm. In the name of Allah, the Most Merciful the Compassionate.

I seek forgiveness from Allah, the Living, and Self-Subsisting Sustainer of all creation. O Allah accept this prayer. O Allah, make mine a prayer that meets with Your acceptance and a request that meets with Your blessing. Indeed You have power over all things.

O Allah, how Perfect You are, we are so blessed to be granted life to worship You, to remember You, to please You and for allowing us to seek Your Majestic Face. We ask for complete *aafiyah* in all our affairs in this World and the Next and we ask for Your Incredible *Rahmah*. We seek Your Immense Pardon in all our affairs, for our constant shortcomings, big and small; known and unknown. Please accept this guide and allow us to please You always, *āmīn*. And Praise be to You, an abundant, beautiful, constant and everlasting praise.

O Allah, send blessings upon our beloved Muhammad ﷺ equal to the number of those who bless him, bless Muhammad ﷺ equal to the number of those who do not bless him, bless Muhammad ﷺ as You command he be blessed, bless Muhammad ﷺ as he loves to be blessed, and bless Muhammad ﷺ as it befits him to be blessed. *āmīn*. Al Fatiha

***

اللَّهُمَّ صَلِّ عَلَىٰ سَيِّدِنَا مُحَمَّدٍ ۞ الْفَاتِحِ لِمَا أُغْلِقَ ۞ وَالْخَاتِمِ لِمَا سَبَقَ ۞ نَاصِرِ الْحَقِّ
بِالْحَقِّ ۞ وَالْهَادِى إِلَىٰ صِرَاطِكَ الْمُسْتَقِيمِ ۞ وَعَلَىٰ آلِهِ حَقَّ قَدْرِهِ وَمِقْدَارِهِ الْعَظِيمِ

O Allah, send blessings upon our master Muhammad ﷺ, the opener to that which is closed, the seal of that which has preceded, the one who gives triumph to the truth by the Truth, the guide unto Your upright path and (send blessings) upon his Family according to his greatness and magnificent rank."

Acknowledgements

Bismi Allāhi al-Raḥmāni al-Raḥīm. In the name of Allah, the Most Merciful the Compassionate.

First and foremost, *al-ḥamdu lillāhi rabbi al-'ālamīn!* Praise be to Allah, the Lord of all the Worlds, who has provided me with the opportunity to complete this book, without His guidance and assistance none of this would have been remotely possible. And to our beloved Prophet Muhammad ﷺ, his family and companions upon whose Seerah and life was an inspiration to carry on forth, who guided and supported me even when there were times I wanted to give up, may immense blessings and peace be upon him and them always, *āmīn*.

I am extremely grateful to my family, blessed sisters and teachers: Ustadha Umm Abdullah, who allowed me to gain a new perspective of the book through fresh eyes and newfound clarity and to Ustadha Saphia — may Allah ﷻ bless and reward them. I would also like to thank sister Khadijah, who introduced me to the publishing world and was the first to display the first edition in her bookstore, may she receive ample reward in abundance. I am very grateful to Kube Publishing and their amazing team for their incredible hard work on the second edition- May you all be rewarded with much goodness *āmīn*. I would also like to thank my sister Zainab who helped me to spread the first edition of the book and guided me gently through the trials I went through, may Allah ﷻ grant her many openings, protect her, guide and illuminate her heart always. To F and S for their continued support: *Jazākum Allāhu khayran,* and to I. And to my beloved husband, may Allah send him beautiful blessings.

I would also like to thank and dedicate this book to my late father, who would sit by my side when I first began my research. And my beautiful mother who through her *du'ā's* helped me to get this far by Allah's Will, and especially to my most precious and sparkling Gem, Fahtima Zahra - the sweetest, kindest, most loving and patient daughter. May Allah ﷻ grant them and my family *Firdaws* and may He unite us with our beautiful beloved *Rasūl Allāh* ﷺ always in the highest stations of everlasting *Jannah, Jannat al-Khuld*, with his beautiful family and the *Sāliḥīn, āmīn yā Rabb!*

Allahumma ṣalli 'ala Sayyidinā Muhammadin wa 'alā Ālih.

Bibliography & References

Al-Basri, H & Mangera, A. Y. (2004). Prayers For Forgiveness. London, UK, White Thread Press.

Al-Hilali, M.D; Khan, M. & International, S. (1999). The Noble Quran. Retrieved from http://www.thenoblequran.com (translation and Quran Arabic text)

Al-Munajjid, M. S. (1997) (General Supervisor). Islamqa.Info. Retrieved from https://islamqa.info/en/23194 (Saheeh Al-Tirmidhi (3477)); (Al Bukhari; Muslim, 1/301); (Al Bukhari, cf. Al-Asqalani, Fathul-Bari, 6/408); (Al Bukhari, cf. Al-Asqalani, Fathul-Bari, 6/407; Muslim, 1/306).

Alim Foundation. (2019) Alim.Org. Retrieved from http://www.alim.org (Qur'anic Arabic text & Transliteration)

Eaalim, Ltd. (2014). "Ibn Yusuf, A. (2007), Salat & Salam, In Praise of Allah's Most Beloved, California, USA, White Thread Press.

Kashi, I. M. & Matzen, U. H. (2014). Al-Quran.Info. Retrieved from http://al-quran.info (transliteration)

Kathir, I. (Tafsir 111.1-5) Retrieved from https://quranx.com/tafsirs/111.4 via (Altafsir.com was commissioned by the Royal Aal al-Bayt Institute for Islamic Thought and developed and maintained by the Integrated Technology Group (2001)

http://al-quran.info/#trans

http://al-quran.info/pages/language/english)

Various. (2007). Muslim Matters.Org Retrieved from https://muslimmatters.org/2012/01/12/add-islamic-phrases-to-your-wordpress-posts/

(*nb for Pg 85): Prophet Muhammad ﷺ read this du'a for protection from Umm Jamil bint Harb, Abu Jahal's wife, source in (Tafsir 111.1-5: https://quranx.com/tafsirs/111.4)